For

Margery Weldon Smith

With my finest regards,

John M. Dorsey, M.D.

Nov. 10, 1969

p. 76 - last ¶ - most important statement. 6/9/72 -
p. 40 - self - fulfillment

xv top: externality inventions of my own mind.
88: Experience . . .

p. 76 power of reasoning vs. self consciousness

"whatever is . . ." 81, top

p. 63
p. 67
p. 77 - dificultly
Study p. 81+82
p. 115

p. 127 - immediate help.

bottom p. 54 - involvee.

George Washington

AMERICAN GOVERNMENT
CONSCIOUS SELF SOVEREIGNTY

John M. Dorsey, M.D.
University Professor
Wayne State University

AMERICAN GOVERNMENT
CONSCIOUS SELF SOVEREIGNTY

"Government is not reason, it is not eloquence—it is force! Like fire, it is a dangerous servant and a fearful master."

George Washington

Published By
Center for Health Education
4421 Woodward Avenue
Detroit, Michigan 48201

Printed by Edwards Brothers, Inc.

Contents

PREFACE

Ever since discovering the sole place of all of my truth as being entirely and only in my self, I have been interested in applying this realization to my study of my personal experience. I have spared my self enormous expenditures of energy by taking the trouble to awaken to the fact that my living is wholly and solely internal, subjective, self contained. To my immense relief this insight enables me to "do something about" my life's complaints, dissatisfactions, or disappointments, of any and every kind and degree. I see that there is only one way for me to change my world, namely by my growing of my self in the direction of the desired modification.

My American government has been the subject of great interest ever since I first learned the meanings named by the two words. This writing represents my continuing effort to uphold my American way of life that, more than any other, represents reverence for the sacred integrity of individual human being. I gratefully vitalize it with spirited patriotic utterances of my freedom loving fellowmen, each scoring this reality: Human individuality is all that can be human.

Thus Charles Evans Hughes finds, "While democracy must have its organization and controls, its vital breath is individual liberty." Theodore Roosevelt exclaims, "The government is us; we are the government, you and I." Woodrow Wilson asks himself and finds the answer, "Just what is it that America stands for? If she stands for one thing more than another it is for the self-sovereignty of self-governing people." James Truslow Adams affirms, "The American Dream . . . has been a dream of being able to grow to the fullest development as man and woman." And so on and on, the defining function of the American is identified with his right and responsibility to cherish his self consciousness. As John Adams referred to his American Constitution in his first Inaugural Address, "What other form of government, indeed, can so well deserve our esteem and love?"

ix

There is properly no other writing, only autobiography. My treatment of the soul of my United States citizenship is intentionally scrupulous. Understandably it must be only the insightful reader who can feel that it reflects his own patriotic sentiment. Certainly it is dearly prized by me as choice aspiration, and I engage in it with as much soul as I can bring to it. My Henry David Thoreau insightfully inquires of his self, "If a man constantly aspires, is he not elevated? Did ever a man try heroism, magnanimity, truth, sincerity, and find that there was not advantage in them—that it was a vain endeavor?"

As might be expected in view of the difficulty every individual must endure now in creating his comprehensive meaning for his whole individuality, the historical evolution of this concept in western culture from its beginning has been a weak version of self autonomy watered down by dilutions of "crude sociologism." Based on his analysis of texts, Bruno Snell brilliantly confirms the view that there is little evidence for a consciously individualized mind in the Homeric era *(The Discovery of the Mind, 1953)*. He finds the first clear appreciation for individuality consciousness in the records of the early lyrists of the sixth century, B. C. He saw development of cherished self realization in man culminating in the fifth century tragedies of Aeschylus and Euripides. Ever since, it has remained the privilege of the freedom loving conscious individualist to work up appreciation for his personalized universality, in the form of honored self sovereignty, as being the *indispensable functional reality* of human government that it actually is. Searching my soul for my highest concern, with an eye for fact, I find it exclusively in my observation of my mind's operation.

In the Preface of his *Talks To Teachers* (1899) my esteemed physician–psychologist William James worded his conscious mindfulness about privacy and incommunicability of the individual mind, noting its *practical consequence:* "the well-known democratic respect for the sacredness of individuality,—is, at any rate, the outward tolerance of whatever is not itself intolerant. These phrases are so familiar that they sound now rather dead in our ears. Once they had a passionate inner meaning. Such a passionate inner meaning they may easily acquire again if the pretension of our nation to inflict its own inner ideals and institutions *vi et armis* upon Orientals should meet with a resistance as obdurate as so far it has been gallant and spirited. Religiously and philosophically, our ancient national doctrine of live and let live may prove to have a far deeper meaning than our people now seem to imagine it to possess."

Study is self experience entirely. By study I can succeed in consciously making my very own the subject I am minding. My reader who can thus grow his self as originally authoring what he reads is thereby augmenting his conscious self knowledge and its consequent lifesaving self appreciation.

INTRODUCTION

"We cannot get to ourselves, there are so many comforts to wade through. Consciousness stops half way."

John S. Dwight

The purpose of this "Appreciation" is to honor with *self felt* consciousness the specific mental healthfulness of my democratic way of life. The only law providing any basis for, and giving any certitude to, government, must be the law of the lawmaker's mind itself. Stated mind awake Novalis (1772–1801), "What I am to understand must develop organically within me; and what I seem to be learning is but mental pabulum, is but a stimulus to the organism."

By "democracy" I mean specifically my glorious American experiment in government of the citizen, by the citizen, and for the citizen, as manifested by my equalitarian doctrine of the Declaration of Independence and by my American ideal of conscious self education for responsible citizenship.

Except for my fellow citizen of Indian blood, every American is of immigrant pioneer stock. My ancestor's self experience with authoritarian disrespect for human individuality, political or religious or both, taught him primary lessons in the dangers of servitude, but out of these perilous beginnings gradually developed my exalted political principle of *self* sovereignty, specifically, of my disciplining my own mental power to rule my own mental reality.

There can be only one real emancipation problem for me, namely that of my freeing my mind from indulging any habit of mine that appears to divide my wholeness of my individuality into one part I can imagine only as my self and another part I can imagine only as not my self. The fearful difficulty about democracy is the laborious mind-reaching which any individual citizen must exert while striving to prepare himself to live conscious self government. Democracy is a government of the individual, by the individual, and for the individual,—and not anything else. Years ago each member of my department of psychiatry conducted a most helpful and most arduous inservice training program in democratic citizenship to the end of escaping authoritarianism in department organization and in medical education. This program demonstrated that education to mature democratic citizenship is education to world citizenship and to free mental health.

I attribute unique health value to the designation, "The American physician." This "hygienic patriotism" may be derived from every physician's proper recognition of the health significance of his American citizenship. The essence of American citizenship is also my recognized teaching ideal: full measured appreciation for the complete sufficiency of the individual. Medical school living represents a critical incidence of civic life, an opportunity for each medical student to further his devotion to the cultivation of *self felt* "equality", *identity*. He *is* his patient living; his patient *is* his own doctor living.

In order to appreciate Britain's abolition of the slave trade in 1807, or Emancipation Act of 1833, or Lincoln's Proclamation of Emancipation of 1863, or the Thirteenth Amendment to the United States Constitution of 1865 outlawing all slavery, or any such Magna Charta of liberation,—each must be meaningful in terms of my very own self-subsisting personal identity, in terms of my empowering my own individual being. It is only in and from my own personal living that any degree of conscious freedom can be experienced by me. To keep alive I must appreciate my life. This appreciation is my supreme virtue and, as John Adams wrote Benjamin Rush in 1808, "How can a man repent of his virtues."

Ralph Waldo Emerson saw wisdom in his necessity thus to declare his allegiance to his own human constitution, "To believe in your own thought . . . is genius." His world of self experience was the recognized realm of his spirit. It is this *conscious* individualism that constitutes the American's unique force of mind, nerving his nonconformity for the persevering self seeing for which he is justly proud. "Socially" acceptable behavior may be easily mistaken for solid citizenship. The self observing scientist, N. R. Campbell, in his *Physics: The Ele-*

ments, recorded, "Ultimately the conclusion cannot be avoided that other persons (if anyone cares to express it so) are merely inventions of my own mind."

By losing sight of my self, I lose my sense of direction. The actual advantage of my democratic government lies in no such abstraction as "a general elevation in the character of the people" or an attainment of a "respectable average of society." Rather, my governing principle of democracy, to the extent that it focuses my attention upon the concrete fact of my human individuality, awakens and develops my liberating consciousness for the discoverable excellence of my own real being. Every form of government that is not clearly recognizable as *self* government, leaves conscious self appreciation to be desired, thus introducing the need for self disesteem.

The founding principle of Jacksonian democracy, "One man is as much worth while as another," was helpful for the American citizen's conceiving a self identity worth living. Seeing clearly that his government exists for him, introduces the American citizen to his difficult obligation to observe his every right of individual freedom with the irrefutable responsibility integral to it. This whole self view requires his purposeful development of a scope of his self identity that is the absolute requirement for conscious self sovereignty. This development is not an outcome of reasoning, but only of his *awakening* to his selfhood and acknowledging it. Mind awakener William James recorded the human tendency to sleep much of one's life away, but rarely am I awake enough to read such glaring news.

Insofar as I cannot awaken to much of my self, I cannot "think much of my self," and I behave accordingly. Thus I seem to require alien control on account of my apparent lack of goodness and greatness. On the other hand, I have never been able to give painless birth to any of my awakening to the illimitable extent of my personal identity. Thomas Jefferson wrote Lafayette (1790), "We are not to expect to be translated from despotism to liberty in a feather bed."

Every kind of government has all of its meaning, or force, in the form of self government. Thus, each communist or fascist too, must live all of *his* own political system. Democratic self government however is unique in that it is the only governmental contrivance devised especially so that each citizen may require himself to be *conscious* that his government is his self government. *Precisely this civic insight is what is ideally meant by "informed electorate."* This study is based chiefly upon the noteworthy fact that the democratic and mental health principles exalt and enforce the same power, *self consciousness,* as their civilizing (individualizing) instrumentality.

My language that is not recognizable as so many names or signs for meanings in my mind, can and does serve to conceal my wholeness and allness from me. Self seeing René Fülöp-Miller writes, "More and more, from the language used in this mechanized century, words which could arouse an image of the organically complete human being tended to go out of use." John Ruskin who wrote such words of self responsibility stirred up fierce hostility in his world. Finally he was compelled to set up his own printing establishment. As Mr. Justice Holmes said, it does seem that "a word is the skin of an idea."

Machiavelli wrote out for his prince many a sage observation, such as this one:

> It must be considered that there is nothing more difficult to carry out, nor more doubtful of success, nor more dangerous to handle, than to initiate a new order of things. For the reformer has enemies in all those who profit by the old order, and only lukewarm defenders in all those who would profit by the new.

He added that to believe anything, it is necessary to have "actual experience of it." To realize actual experience of anything, it is necessary for me to *see* that I am living it.*

"What a great number of people think," is an abstraction of limited self helpfulness. "What each man thinks," or "What I think," is a concrete view which can bear investigation. The abstract, "A great number of minds," cannot pass for the concrete, *One real mind.* The real culture of the real individual cannot be equated with the illusional individuality of the imag-

*Cf., my *A Psychoanalytic Appreciation of American Government.* The American Imago, Vol. 18, No. 3, Fall, 1961.

ined cult. "Consensus of opinion" rules despotically where opinion of consensus is repressed. My education must be clearly observable as a self discovery, if it is to contribute most to the creation of my government clearly observable as self government, if it is to arouse the vital spiritual dimension of my human being. James Harvey Robinson described need for this cherishable mind consciousness well: "The little word *my* is the most important one in all human affairs, and properly to reckon with it is the beginning of wisdom. It has the same force whether it is my dinner, my dog, and my house, or my faith, my country, and my God."

Appreciation for my self sovereignty can be furthered only by my *difficultly* extending my realization of the unbounded range of my self identity. *Conscious* freedom is the creation only of hard work of self awakening. In his uniquely sane speech in behalf of the U. S. O., 1941, John D. Rockefeller, Jr., began a sequence of self binding beliefs stressing the primary significance of his responsible self orientation, "I believe in the supreme worth of the individual and in his right to life, liberty, and the pursuit of happiness." Such enlightened selfishness results in a morality of self discipline, teaching that virtue is a name for free mindedness and vice is a name for enslaved self identity.

My "neighbor" *is* made up of meanings in and of my self, hence loving "him" is expressing my love for that much of my own life. *My* "enemy" is made up of meanings in and of my self, hence loving "him" is expressing my love for that much of my own life. Each of these as well as every other demonstrable fact of my life recorded in the following pages is the subject of greatest immediate concern for me. *I record whatever conception is important for me in thousands of different ways. Furthermore I find that whatever conception I cannot state in numerous ways is one about which I must observe: I care to know little about it.*

John Adams

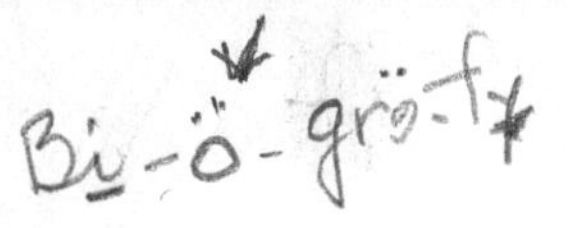

DEMOCRATIC EDUCATION

"Laws and institutions must go hand in hand with the progress of the human mind."

Thomas Jefferson

The primary political truth is this: The consciously complete American citizen is one who sees all that he learns about "government" as being developments of his own mind. He observes that *he* must create every "coercive" agency, or force, of meaning for him. *E Pluribus Unum* is his motto, as it is the motto of his country. His recognition of his all-inclusive self possession prevents his "memorizing factual data of civics" as constituting citizenship training. Memorizing which is accomplished at the cost of self forgetting is a hideous caricature of education.

The illusion of "communicating" democratic principles cannot pass as education for democratic living. Dictionaries are of little help in clarifying the definition of any kind of "teaching." It will probable be many centuries before the superstition that language enables "communication," can be renounced. Truth is the product of autobiography only. A man's history as to how he has *consciously* cherished his autonomy, reveals to his self the extent of sincerity in his living. By habitual awareness that my life makes all of my world, I can enjoy—in Jefferson's words—"the illimitable freedom of the human mind to explore and expose every subject susceptible of its contemplation."

Certainly one cannot enable another to see the necessity for self government. A teacher cannot enable his pupil to see *that* life necessity, any more than he can do his pupil's breathing for him. Yet, only a consciousness for learning which is recognizable as an extension of self awareness, is most suitable to the dignity of the human mind.

Wendell L. Wilkie proudly proclaimed, "The Constitution does not provide for first and second class citizens." Certainly as any student of his human constitution must attest, one mind cannot provide for self and "not-self" interests. I *am* my fellow-man. That single standard realization of my self identity is my source of my morality.

The insightful teacher of conscious self government must be personally interested in having his pupil awaken to the benefits of conscious self government. A teacher may and does say what he knows about democracy, but he grows his speaking exclusively as his self development. His pupil may have (hear) his teacher say what he knows about democracy, but he grows his "hearing" too as an extension of his own selfhood. Whether or not a pupil decides to try to live his teacher's spoken knowledge wholly as his accepted view, is a matter which is entirely up to the individual pupil. Upon this decision, however, rests any meaning of the concept "successful teaching." It is to be noted that every educational triumph is that of the learner only. The insightful teacher finds his educational triumph in seeing his pupil as thus educating his self to conscious self sovereignty.

Only to the extent that I have difficultly cultivated my self identity, can I appreciate the motto, "That government is best which governs least." Only to the extent that I have developed my self responsibility as Thoreau did his, can I safely rely on such conscious self reliance as, "For government is an expedient by which men would fain succeed in letting one another alone."

That self wise English statesman, John Bright, wished that the young Englishman would study his American authors, and observed to a renowned American, "I read your poets in preference to ours, not because they are greater poets, but because they are greater citizens. Your Bryant, your Longfellow, your Whittier, and your Lowell take part in a common life of the nation, and are all better poets because they are completer men."

Thornton Wilder minds, "All literature is one expression of one human life-experience." A complete, full grown, American citizen is necessarily a man of peace, and he is wise to the fact that democratic government provides a peaceful method for every needed reform. Jefferson dearly and properly prided himself in the fact that his administration was a war free one.

Exactly the opposite of Jefferson's intention, Does the Ameri-

can pupil tend to live his public schooling to the end that he see
little or no self in it? Does he consummate his educational
living by not even missing his appreciation of his own creaturehood in it? Does the American pupil tend to consider education
as an opportunity to learn as much as possible about "somebody
else" and "something else?" Such unconscious self experience
cannot prepare him for assuming his natural right of conscious
self government. On the contrary, by disciplining his mind in self
unconsciousness he prepares himself to require a minimum of
concious self government. *For the insightful American educator
no greater danger exists than that this enslaving kind of schooling by the American citizen be overlooked any longer.*

The only possible way to teach Jefferson or Shakespeare
safely or sanely, is for the educator to be aware that he is growing his own Jefferson or Shakespeare meanings, by consciously
cultivating the thoughts and feelings in himself which he imag-
ines his Jefferson or Shakespeare to have. "This earth," cried
Thoreau, "which is spread out like a map around me, is but the
lining of my inmost soul exposed," and, "In me is the sucker
that I see," and of Walden Pond,

<blockquote>
"I am its stony shore,
And the breeze that passes o'er."
</blockquote>

Extravagant expectations followed American legislation
guaranteeing civic freedom. Jefferson hoped that public schooling would be all that would be necessary for the freeborn child to
develop his mind with self consciousness, so that he might
thereby grow the proper esteem for his human greatness. However, insightful experience demonstrates man's preferred self
ignorance as an essential device for his maintaining whatever
sense of mental equilibrium (sense of self identity) he has, pend-
ing his growing his *willingness* to observe his growing knowledge
as self knowledge. I *am* my experience I dislike, but that is hard
to see.

To be greatly self perceptive is the greatest human development. I honor my world most by seeing my identity in it. None
but my selfish eyes can see me as I am, as my everyone and

3

everything. Every self observation becomes a fresh integration of truth, never lessening but ever enlarging my life's meanings.

My beloved physician William Osler esteemed his self insistent Emerson highly indeed, recommending to his medical students the study of that great all-American seer's works as healthy psychological exercise. From my Emerson's Journal V page 179, I excerpt the following humane definition of Science: "The perception of identity is a good mercury of the progress of the mind. I talk with very accomplished persons who betray instantly that they are strangers in nature. The cloud, the tree, the sod, the cat, are not theirs, have nothing of them. They are visitors in the world, and all the proceedings and events are alien, immeasurable, and across a great gulf. The poet, the true naturalist, for example, domesticates himself in nature with a sense of strict consanguinity. His own blood is in the rose and the apple-tree. This is true science." Thus Emerson recorded his prescription for his own peaceful human development: conscious mental integration. Applying this oneness insight to his world's affairs, Crane Brinton writing upon *The Chances For A World State,* claims, "First of all, it is certain that we of Western society have never, in our five thousand years of recorded history, kept peace for long within an area save by bringing that area within the authority of a single government."

In the American Association of University Professors Bulletin,* Donald Faulkner's study, *Democracy In Higher Education,* notes:

"Many advanced thinkers in America and in other sections of the world consider civilization's only hope to lie in a more conscientious effort to understand and to make democracy work, and not in bombs and space ships, not even in an international organization backed by a world police force. That is, the world must find a more sincere, a more direct and consistent social and political organization than any so-called democracy has yet developed. This, we Americans all contend, is our nation's chief business. We, the teachers of America, hold it just as strongly to be the urgent task and the opportunity of educa-

*Summer Issue, Volume 45, No. 2, June 1959.

tion." However, everyone to his taste. Reluctant to practice conscious self education in order to become consciously self enduring for self sovereignty, it is understandable if I resist, quoting my Samuel Johnson to the effect that I need not eat the whole ox to tell "if the meat be tough." However it is also understandable if I choose to quote my Alfred E. Smith, "All the ills of democracy can be cured by more democracy."

Thomas Jefferson saw that each American citizen must educate himself to become capable of declared self government. He regarded ignorance as "that greatest enemy of man's freedom and happiness." In Bernard Mayo's words, "He fully, and passionately, subscribed to the view that what happens to American education will eventually happen to the American nation . . . His educational plans were adopted by other states, and were so influential that they have been called 'the charter of the American public school system.' "

My language is of primary helpfulness in my self exploration called "education." By using my words for each of my mind's actions I succeed in naming the innumerable modifications and infinite variety of my life's meaning. It is most important for me to understand that I must consciously control this self naming faculty of mine or it certainly will soon appear to be controlling me. My language has behind it my particular way of using my mind. Only in my awakening of this realistic language consciousness do I begin to be aware of my life's marvelous possibilities.

My American education needs constant reforming in the specific direction of my *seeing* my every experience as setting me free to develop my latent capacity. The only possible authority in my education is my mind's awakening to its vitality. The psychology from which I deduce my political philosophy is consciously all my own. I find my fellowman also wants to be let alone, but it appears that he too must set his self free, in the only way possible, by his awakening to his truth that he *is* a free one and only one.

Free mindedness is my only possible real freedom. My authoritarian experience, from the nursery on, lulls to sleep my power to awaken to my need for conscious self government. *In my work I observe how every person grows life appreciation only in terms of his discovering the wonderfulness of his own life through his self realization.* Discipline in living self consciously, is the most helpful inservice training experience for my every American teacher. Jefferson's program of free public education had as a chief purpose the safeguarding of democracy from being a breeding ground of demagogues. Its extension is truly wonderful provided that it stands for each pupil's educating his self about his self. As Bishop J. L. Spalding recognized, "Only they have come of age who have learned how to educate themselves."

The question I must ever ask my self is, What is my American child doing to his mind with his education? Is he building his sense of self identity with it so that he can become capable of devotion to his world? Is he taking the trouble to heed that all of his knowledge is self knowledge? Is he awakening to *his* self world insightfully? My answer to my self questioning is always a provoking one. I find my child "learning" that nothing is really real that is not quantifiable; that "outward" tangible consequence is what counts; that "external" worldliness is the desirable aim of life; that "individuality" must stand for narrow selfishness and morbid egotism; that personal identity can exist only at the expense of the "general good;" and on and on, all at the cost of conscious self responsibility.

And why do I consider my awareness for my human individuality to be my greatest good? Merely since I recognize that the *only* good I can observe is revealed in my self by my self and of my self. I recognize that I can revere my individuality only to the extent that I can discover its worth. This observable and demonstrable fact clearly and fully explains my (including my fellowman's) conduct of life.

In the *Law of Love and the Law of Violence,* Leo Tolstoy recorded:

> From the day when the first members of councils placed exterior authority higher than interior, that is to say, recognized the decisions of men united in councils as more important and more sacred than reason and conscience; on that day began lies that caused the loss of

millions of human beings and which continue their unhappy work to the present day.

As philosopher or scientist I must acknowledge the desirability in testing any possible utterance I can make with my principle of verifiability. I ask my self, Verifiable by what? Nothing but my self experience can verify its own being. As philosopher, any proposition I cannot verify may be classified as "absurd." However I can and do fully verify my idea, or thought, or view, or mental production of any kind, merely by heedfully observing it as consisting of the reality, or truth, or substantial force of my organic being. *Any* mental event such as my thinking, or observing, or sensing, or whatever, *is* always a forceful reality of my life. It is only my living it that can "hypostatize" it.

I have always enjoyed an access of mighty conscious helpfulness whenever I learned (awakened) sufficient conscious self knowledge to use my mind in any additional way. Also every latest addition has ever seemed a final culmination of my mental development, even though it always proved itself to be merely one event in an ongoing process.

My arousing my awareness to appreciate the fact that *my* world is all and entirely a world of my mind has enabled me to practice hard at using my mental power to please my self, to make me feel my goodness at will, to create for my self my heart's desire, to conceive my heaven or utopia or ideal world according to my clearly personal specifications. Before exciting my mind with responsibility for, and voluntary access to, this amazing resourcefulness, as does nearly everyone of my world, I also tended to fear such a world-making function as a sign of mental "deviation" rather than as the essential source of sanity it really is. To illustrate, I now see clearly that for me as a white to be able to recognize my black living as all mine that *only* I can ever experience and regulate to suit my self, or as a black to be able to recognize my white living as all mine that *only* I can ever experience and regulate to suit my self, is now most critically needed functioning of my mind. However I, including my black and white fellowman, must either keep willing to try to become wide awake to my world of self, or continue to suffer self hatred, self anger, and other painful self frustration on account of expecting "someone else" to be able to make my life a satisfying one for me. I find no other way to recognize my freedom except by thus *seeing* my self free.

I am *absolutely* my self. I make this declaration of independence knowing that my several Supreme Court Justices of the United States not very long ago justly "handed down" a thought provoking statement that "nothing is more certain in modern society than the principle that there are no absolutes." The abstraction "modern society" is entirely a conception of the concrete *individual*. I state to my self, I can experience and observe nothing at all certain or uncertain except the individuations of my absolute individuality. Only I *can* make *my* world safe for my experiencing and observing my conscious self government. My somebody else cannot do that or anything else for me. He can and must do all of it for his self if he will ever achieve enjoyment of the potential wonder, freedom, independence, and worldfulness inherent in his American citizenship.

Conscious souled Ralph Waldo Emerson considered nothing mightier than an idea whose time has finally arrived. The idea that the best a human being can do is *consciously to work his mind* is not new in nature but certainly it demands and deserves its turn.

DEMOCRATIC LEADERSHIP

"The republican is the only form of government which is not eternally at open or secret war with the rights of mankind."

Thomas Jefferson

The American chief executive, the President of the United States, is supreme political officer, and while in office is national head but not congressional leader of his party. The Presidency provides opportunity for the strongest kind of human mind, the kind capable of the greatest capacity for observing and extending its personal identity. Ideally each American citizen must be able to see his president within, as his own life, not as "someone" bigger or greater than his self. Presidential ability to delegate, coordinate and direct nationally and internationally, is fundamental. *Conscious* self possession, self reliance, independence, imagination, available will power, workableness, appreciation for human life enabling worldful humaneness—*each a product of the discipline of self consciousness and a democratic ideal*—are qualities of presidential timber.

That person can and does "hold office," from president to precinct committeeeman, who can liberally afford the self tolerance required to seem "popular." By seeming "popular" I mean specifically: living his constituent willingly (consciously) as his own living of his constituent, and seeing his constituent live his democratic official willingly (consciously) as his own democratic officer. That politician or statesman is most "popular" who is capable of growing and recognizing (as his) the most individual citizen identities in his own life. He creates and acknowledges each of his fellow citizens as an entified existent of his life, as an individuation of his individuality. One thing sure, the official life of a democratic leader exploiting a "cleaner-than-thou" attitude towards his electorate, is bound to be a short one.

Democratic process by its very nature ideally insures continuance of humaneness, for it bases itself entirely where it really is to be found, namely, in the mind of the individual citizen. Even my brilliant Thomas Carlyle of 19th Century England found democracy inseparable from mediocrity. Possible he was not considering 1) the allness of his individuality and 2) the health and happiness created by such true (full measured) self consciousness. "Mediocrity" can be a most cruel word with which the hurt mind may be expressing its "worthier-than-thou" symptoms. Despite its admitted "mediocrity," my democratic government is the best ever devised for me to create my appreciation for my individuality.

Chief Justice Charles E. Hughes created a view, of vital concern now, "The question today is whether we have enough of the old spirit which gave us our institutions, to save them from being overwhelmed." He referred to the *spirited* conceptions of the individual, called the Declaration, Constitution, and Bill of Rights.

One sightless criticism of democracy is that it does not guarantee the best "leadership of the people." Contrary to the view of everyone inexperienced in conscious self government, no citizen's chance of life liberty and pursuit of happiness is enhanced by any supreme leadership of any "other man" known as a "great democrat." "Supreme leadership of somebody else," can never represent the true democratic way of life. Carl Sandburg quotes "Bill Green's point: New Salem neighborhood has no principal citizen; every man there is a principal citizen."

Unquestionably, man's development as a democratic citizen is by far his most difficult governmental development. It is a relatively easy matter to grow one's self as the loyal subject of a king, or as a very important cog in the very important wheel of the very important commune. Cultivating the strength of mind which enables him to see himself as the author of his liberty, as the creator of his being, as the founder of his country, as the maker of his world,—only his conscious freedom to evolve and awaken to his comprehensive personal identity so that he can cherish his self sovereignty, outfits the democratic elector for this kind of life appreciation.

It is my obscuration to say, "The people" represent the supreme power in democratic government. "The people," is all and only my precious self view, my personified abstraction in my mind. Every individual creates his own cult, or party. The foundation upon which my democratic testament rests is deeper than rejected selfness called "the people." This foundation goes down to the recognition of my Human Individuality in its particularized allness. "The world is nothing, man is all," was Emerson's ideality. Of such self insight is constituted real political genius.

Comprehensively conceived human individuality is neither didactic nor dogmatic. It cannot come under the category of means. It offers no help to an "outside" world, being worldwide in its own extent. It is not to be confused therefore with any doctrinaire individualism which is not at the same time recognizable as cosmopolitanism. As a valid theory of society, it sees all of "society" as only meaning in the given mind creating it. Elmer Davis briefs its world consequence, "One world or none, say the atomic scientists." After studying the helpfulness in self appreciation in 1790, Johann Gottlieb Fichte recorded, "My scheming mind has found rest at last . . . I concern myself more with my own being."

John Buchan (Lord Tweedsmuir) described American Democracy as "the conscious work of men's hands." His further description might almost as well be applied to conscious mental integration, "the supreme example of a federation in being, a federation which recognizes the rights and individuality of the parts, but accepts the overriding interests of the whole." Each citizen is all of his own "people," and "people" cannot have any "say" in government. Edmund Burke, even though he too tried to lump one individual with another, did somewhat recognize government to be a product of each individual: "There never was for any long time a corrupt representation of virtuous people, or a mean, sluggish, careless people that ever had a good government of any force." No matter how I consider any matter, the one fact remains: I created the consideration. Thus I respect the growth and freedom of my conscious nature.

Every citizen is his own government. May that life-giving and life satisfying truth come to his consciousness. To this end political science, recognized as a self development of the political scientist, can be most helpful. Without it the individual must resign his right to be aware that he is directing his own life. Each American citizen is his own "many," not one of many, and it is his political duty to uphold that proposition. Little wonder that Hegel, who consistently held self consciousness to be a painful mark of frustration and helpfulness, attributed to "the State" the self-evident rights of man and conceived freedom as a "social" phenomenon. The painful observation must be made that Marx, Lenin, Engels, or every "materialist" (except each one whose "material" is consciously mental) must restrict his self grievously in the ever helpful use of self consciousness. It is by recognizing my fellowman as being integral to the wholeness of my inner being that I cultivate my appreciation for my so-called "communal" self.

Another fact which is well worth most careful consideration is this: Rarely, if ever, has the truth been recognized that the solipsistic life orientation can deny nothing, for to do so would be to deny part of its own existence. Certainly there must exist as many definitions for a term as there are ones who take the trouble to define it. I use the literal meaning of solipsism: one's self alone. By asserting my life to be my intrinsic life alone I necessarily describe my self as a solipsist, as one who acknowledges that he and only he lives whatever he lives. Practicing this natural process of acknowledging my self realization I cannot but gradually awaken to the comprehensive truth of my capacity for conscious cosmic being, for sensing my responsibility for my own created world of my self, the ideal consequence of conscious self education. My educational alternative to recognizing my learning as my responsible living is that dormant mental sensibility known as "pedantry." Distrust of my human nature is my only possible kind of distrust, but it can exist in innumerable and unrecognizable forms. I have had to resort to its dogmatic direction often for immediate relief. It is my discipline of conscious self freedom that provides my safe and sane social living.

As a rule, solipsism is briefly dismissed with the notion that it denies the existence of "external reality." This it does not and cannot do, despite Lenin's claim that it does. The solipsistic position was conspicuously foreign to Lenin's "materialistic" way of thinking. The subjectivism of insightful individuality can never become a serious philosophical or political position until it first becomes psychologically obvious. It is true, however, that one cannot but wonder if the all-important oneness of human individuality is not a suppressed, rather than negated, assumption of the communist as of every other non-democratic organizer. The reality of practice sets up the truth of individuality and shows up the fiction of "society." It demonstrates that it is necessary to extend self consciousness in order to extend good will and love. This self conscious living of life is strenuous work.

Alfred North Whitehead said, "Ideas won't keep. Something must be done about them. The idea must constantly be seen in some new aspect. Some element of novelty must be brought into it freshly from time to time." Certainly I find that eternal self vigilance is the price I must pay for enjoying my only freedom, my mental freedom. There is no self betrayal while imagination for this reality is agile. I can understand only whatever I can imaginatively observe in my mind. Larger self consciousness only can reveal all ignorance and corruption as shortsighted self help. Acknowledged self identity is the supreme help.

Democratic tests of leadership are the only possible foolproof ones. A democratic demagogue is preferable to a benevolent despot in the all-important sense that democracy keeps open the possibility of later developments of conscious self sovereignty. Democratic politics described as becoming "too corrupt, too debased, to soil the hands of the upright citizen," are really the necessary democratic developments with which the "upright citizen" must discover for himself his own unreadiness for conscious self government and democratic living. Of Grover Cleveland, Henry L. Mencken wrote, "He came into office his own man, and he went out without yielding anything of that self sufficient character."

Historian Guglielmo Ferrero records,

Authority comes from above . . . legitimacy comes from below. (This) . . . explains why democracy cannot be legitimized without an internal spiritual unity if all the people are not in agreement both on the principle of legitimacy and on the great moral and religious principles of life. If that unity does not exist, the right of opposition becomes the battleground for a struggle to the death.

AMERICAN CITIZENSHIP IN THE MAKING

> "I count life just a stuff
> To try the soul's strength on, educe the man."
>
> Browning

This section treats of the sole source, substance and seat of my conscious American government: my self.

It seems clearly understandable to me that the most helpful making of my mind depends entirely upon the way it educates itself. My seeing my experience in this all-important respect brings up the question of what constitutes "most helpful" mentality. The ready answer is: self conscious mentality, lively subjectivity, vitally appreciated responsible individuality, insightful self realization, recognizable creative imagination,—every kind of observable life affirmation in duly esteemed personal integration.

This one desirable goal of my self education, my appreciation for my personal identity, specifies the nature of the educational process best designed to achieve it. I must awaken to my self knowledge with unremitting concern for my inviolable integrity. My every lesson must be understood as my self creation. My learning of my world must be identical with my discovery of the comprehensiveness of my unique individuality. All of my discipline in altruism (love of my fellowman, concern for human welfare, civic responsibility, and the like) must be appreciated as enlightened self fulfillment. My knowledge must be heeded as self knowledge. My growth of meaning of any kind must be collated with my every other kind of personal growth. Whatever I find out about my world must be oriented directly as my self possession. I must learn to treat my fellowman as myself, for (my) he is I.

Whatever is alive is growing itself only. This self growth is called "organic development." All I can be is the existence I become. All of my doing is nothing but my being. I do what I am; I am what I do. My every activity is a force of my being, called "biological process." My every such vital energy may proceed without great resistance, or it may have to modify itself in varying degree to adapt itself to its necessity. The science of "pathology" deals with the consequent struggling physiological processes of my constitution. The growth of my vocabulary undergoes innumerable vicissitudes involving continuing modification. As far as self respect is concerned, its chief alteration results in its clearly naming my developing *meaning* for my individuality.

My every meaning of any kind, indeed whatever I live, *is* a creation of my individuality. However, I must discipline my mental development in a most specific direction in order to build up my *conscious* meaning for the allness nature of my individuality. My growing comprehensive understanding for my intact wholeness, for my inviolable unity, requires most strenuous purposeful mental effort. Hence, adequate appreciation for the real extent of my "Man's estate" is most rarely achieved. Consequently the idea of the cheapness of human (individual) life sets up, with all of its train of human (individual) ordeal. I personally depreciate the divinity of my human nature exactly to the extent that I help myself by consciously disowning any of my life experience as being personally my own. My impersonalism is my only possible basis for my atheism, or "inhumanity."

The more primitive my mind, the less its conscious self identity contains its divinity meanings, or any other of its meanings. Development of my conscious love of life varies directly with how much of my experience I can succeed in seeing as personally life worthy. I may measure my personal appreciation for my self growth in inverse proportion to my appreciation for its "popularity."

A life of impersonalism is as close as I can get to living death. In that sense, helping my self by consciously disowning any of my experience, amounts to focal suicide. Conversely, personally acknowledging experience I formerly repudiated as not mine, amounts to my personally coming alive. What I unwittingly mean by "fear of death" must be fear associated with arousing my *living* of the idea of dying. There is no death in life. Death itself cannot be a living experience. What I mean by it may be my wish to terminate living, a wish my everyone may vaguely indulge without realizing it clearly.

Whenever I live pain or unhappiness of any kind, I am already unconsciously wishing to stop it and its associated precious living, for I cannot recognize their lifesaving importance. *My emotion is to my whole mind what pain or pleasure is to my mind's body.* Therefore my "emotional appreciation," as all of my judgment and reasoning and every other mental activity, is biologically subordinate to my crowning glory, my self consciousness. Certainly unless I can awaken enough to see the biological wisdom in my pain and all unhappiness, I must be tempted to live pessimistically. Misery in all of its manifestations is often shortsightedly described as "immedicable." Immedicable it is, fortunately, for it is itself the constitutional medicine of man. Man's capacity for distress is indispensable, warning him about how his way of using his mind is endangering his existence, and counselling him about how to extend his understanding of the lifesaving helpfulness of his unhappy feelings so that he can recognize his need to alter his self's culture desirably.

Unless I take the trouble to observe what my every word means, in terms of *my* existence the meaning names, I must go on living as if my words can do my thinking for me. This mental condition, of allowing my language to appear to subject me to it, may exist without my ever finding it out. It produces signs and symptoms of unhappiness, but I am rarely able to interpret them as lifesaving indicators.

My first self created language of my mind establishes itself without my realizing adequately either that I am creating it by my self or that it can name only meanings about my self. Quite the contrary. I must consequently create my two language illusions. The one deceives me to judge I am "receiving" my language skill from my teacher. The other deceives me to judge that nearly all of my language refers, not to my meaning for the world of my self but rather, to my meaning for an "external" world. By overlooking the fact that I teach my self my words to help me understand myself, my language of my self, I can hide from my conscious mind precious consolation derivable only from my sensing my *whole* being. The "remedy" for this "malady" of self disesteem, responsible for all disguised or undisguised suicide or homicide, cannot be my esteem or love or worship for "another," for that "altruism" can be possible only as unconscious self appreciation.

As my Emerson describes it, "A strong common sense, which is not easy to unseat or disturb, marks the English mind for a thousand years." In his beautiful essay *Literature,* he goes on to point out that "exactitude of mind" is furthered by a choice of words clearly expressive of the nature of the person doing the choosing: "This mental materialism makes the value of English transcendental genius" whose dynamic brain hurled off his words "as the revolving stone hurls off scraps of grit . . . His mind must stand on a fact."

The Oriental predecessor of the ancient Greek represented his god as a phantastic animal, or composite man and animal. Then the human nature loving Greek made his god in his own image. It remains for *self conscious* man to observe that *he is* the only God he can know anything about. I regularly observe: It is divine to be my self, but it is human for me to overlook it. To be insensitive for any of my living sets a limit to my ability to take care of my self. I am mindful of my Thoreau's observing, "The laws of the universe are not indifferent *but are forever on the side of the most sensitive."*

For understanding my fearful language predicament that sets up and maintains my self unawareness, I help myself by a simple and striking illustration. My body can support only limited weight while I am growing up. I do not expect an infant or young child to lift a heavy burden an older child can. Also, I must discipline my body in order to become a "weight lifter." Just so, as an infant I am unable to assume heavy conscious responsibility for being my self. My self consciousness is my focusing my attention upon my meaning for my own existence. This *acknowledging* responsibility for being my self is the heaviest kind of mental weight. Therefore it is hardly ever adopted as a way of life. However, its absence accounts for the craving for anonymity characteristic of the mobster, organization man, dictator, and every other individual who cannot live his meaning for *his* fellowman as an individuation of his own self's meaning. Its presence accounts for any and all appreciation for human individuality. *What about that!* I say to my self.

My concept of my self enjoys accelerated growth as my locomotion unceremoniously introduces me to one after another discrete self of my world. Especially on account of my professional work's necessitating my identifying my self in extremes of my human individualism, I have disciplined my mind in conscious mental weight lifting. The heaviest weight of all is: *seeing my personal identity in whatever I experience.* All love of adventure is based on courageous, expectant self development.

I see my fellowman, each one, as truly wonderful. However, I see each one varying as I do in his disciplined power to make his self *conscious* for his wonderfulness. My meliorative term can be used for conscious self repudiation, quite as can my pejorative term. Thus I can exclude from my conscious self identity not only whatever I associate with dislike but also whatever I associate with love or adoration. I may then not include either my mate or my maker in my conscious self appreciation.

I honor my choice design for living, my gradually building up the required conscious mental tolerance to call my world my own and my all my world, as my difficult and correspondingly rewarding *scholarly* education of my mind. It is most self enriching experience to be able to observe, "I *am* all of my world; I can 'have' nothing of an 'external' world." Ancient Aristotle observes, "It is not wealth but character that lasts," and "Man's happiness consists in the free exercise of his highest faculties." My free consecration to consciousness for my personal life, is my functioning that subsumes all other sources of self satisfaction.

If I temporarily renounce my tremendous temptation to personify my living in such a term as "Government," and study the factuality involved in my irresponsible use of that word, I find nothing but the personifier. As I see it, too much cannot be made over this plain and easily recognizable truth. Actually, however, it is hard work to make much over it. Although my unheeding it amounts really to a kind of word delirium or a semantic psychosis, I regularly overlook the limited advantage in this kind of talk, as if it might be of little or no consequence. Despite my determined persistent efforts to make myself aware of my responsibility for its every meaning, my own mind continues to suffer definite habit deterioration based upon easy unnoticed verbal addictions.

Compounding personifications, I can talk or write such expressions as "the State," "The United States," "American government," and so on and on, without considering my own self as at all conspicuous in such a display, although the only abiding fact in all of it *is* entirely myself. Nevertheless, rarely do I begin or end my scientific exposition with the real truth that it is all and only about me. Quite the contrary notion is implied, namely, that I am able to talk about somebody else or something else or some place else. Furthermore, during such self unconscious talking or writing I am apt to suffer no sense of guilt, no feeling of misrepresenting factuality, no appreciation that my entire production is other than "the impersonal externality" I make it appear to be, e.g., "*the* President," "yesterday's meeting," *the* "family," "home," "school," "church," "city hall," "community," "stock exchange," or *the* whatever.

The nature of education is determined by perceptive human nature, that is, by the given individual's sensibility. Human nature belongs only to each (one) intact whole human being. To the extent that I can observe my *intact* wholeness I do not need to account for any of my living on the basis of somebody or something other than myself. However, once I cannot acknowledge *any* of my living as being my own, I must start dividing my mind into what I can see and call "I," and what I see and call "not-I."

My "educability" is no exception to my indivisible individuality. My learning is nothing but my own awakening to the meaning of my own self experience. However, if I cannot recognize my living of my learning experience as being my own, I must consider it as being foreign to me, and account for my knowing about it on the basis of being "influenced" by an alien authority. Painful (any unhappy) living is apt to be thus classified as "Not-I."

Learning, as all else human, is always a given mind's activity only. The individual is the sufficient source of whatsoever that can have meaning for him. If consciously or unconsciously I do not see to it that I secure (become) my air to breathe, water to drink, and food to eat, I must die. Usually it looks as if somebody else can serve me, or assist me somehow, but that "seeming" is dispelled as I acknowledge my "somebody else" as mine.

I am the unity of all of my reality, but my self consciousness too rarely includes even a glimpse of this all-important comprehensiveness of mine. The cost I must pay for helping myself by denying or ignoring that I am whatever I dislike, is my conscious unwillingness to attend to my very own difficult living so that I can take care of it kindly.

Right now my "worldly" man is raging mad over phantom problems traceable directly to each individual's setting up innumerable so-called "foreign" meanings in his own mind to which he attributes immense power which is really all and only his own. Nearly everyone I live ("world diplomat," "peace delegate," "patriotic statesman," "civic leader," included) seems to rely upon his plurals, personifications and pejorative terms, quite as if they might be dependable for keeping him out of trouble instead of surely getting him in it deeper and deeper. My reading of every dictionary and encyclopedia of my world just fans the flame of my delusional impersonalism, unless I heed cautiously that *my* reading personalizes me only.

As I heed the monstrous results for my world effected by such pejorative words as "barbarian," "savage," "crime," "inferior," "enemy," "inhuman" (on and on), I am impelled to work hard and fast to establish my only possible sane world language, my language of self. Again, I observe the term "race" which has no existence whatever except in the mind of the person creating and using it, and consider the enormous suffering of my fellowman traceable directly to its delusional force. I see clearly how this word, made up all and only of me and by me, can appear to exclude its creator.

My only "integration" that can possibly have any real meaning is the absolute inviolable oneness of my mind. My only "segregation" that can possibly have any real meaning is the result of my inability to call all of my mind my own, thus creating an imaginary schism "separating" my living I can recognize and be responsible for, from my living I must repudiate and seem irresponsible for. "Separation" is always illusional, implying duality or plurality rather than unity. Whatever is *wholly* is.

What can my conception "man" or "God" or "angel" or "devil" or "world" or whatever, be but (as the term "conception" implies) my very own self made creation. Government can do nothing. It has no force but that of a single meaning in a single mind. It has no senses, no energy, no life whatsoever of its own. Plato observed the allness of his being in his assertion, Only the mind is beautiful,—not Art. "Religion" is equally lifeless except as a term owing all of its meaning to the individual mind conceiving it. "Psychology" has no mind of its own. "Reality" has absolutely no existence except that which one's mind makes for it. "Philosophy" has no love of wisdom in its ten letters. The only energy or love or consequence in any word or combination of words I use is entirely and only an expression of my living of my self consequence. My auxiliary verb "to have" is divisive, upholding the illusion and delusion of objectivity; "to be" is unitive, duly supporting subjectivity. I "have" nothing; I *am* my everything.

How apparently helpful but really impossible are my seemingly irresponsible self expressions like,

> The individual is a member of Society.
> The growing insight of our age.
> The reflective method of philosophy.
> The State will administer justice.
> Powerful organizations are reaching for power.
> In the interest of the great masses of the people.

Innumerable word sequences such as these ignore all that gives them any consequence at all, namely the nature of the person in whom they have all of their meaning, in my instance my acknowledged self. Nevertheless, nearly all of the governmental literature of my world consists of such self unconsciousness of its author. My custom has made this kind of self deceptive diction acceptable, even seem "scholarly." As everyone else of my world, I tend to judge my established pedagogy as quite helpless for relieving me of my necessity for mental trouble necessarily issuing in "disorder," including war.

Certainly I enjoy some degree of knowing that my "disorder" cannot occur except I discipline my self specifically to it; that I must train my self thoroughly to conduct my life either irresponsibly or responsibily; that all of my true morality or immorality has come from educating my will to it. I also know to some extent that my self knowledge is thorough only when I can use it at will for the interest of my whole self. My chief source of trouble lies in my addictions to so-called "common sense" attitudes favoring my soft cheap unadventurous living, favoring my ignoring my tremendous potentiality, favoring my valuing living as a settling down to routine rather than settling up of my human obligations. In other words, I am in constant need of consciously drilling my self to recognize my self,—my only possible sane "education."

It requires much of my courage to consider the dread consequence in the resulting chain of events, whenever I put in sequence these specific realizations: 1) An unused function is the heaviest kind of life burden; 2) Self consciousness, man's crowning glory, is his supreme mental function; and 3) My mind's capacity for self consciousness is insufficiently exalted as theory or experienced in practice, even while I seem awake.

When I reduce the above self observation to a simple statement it means: only my living self heedully is compatible with the law of my human constitution. This is a sharp contrast to the view that reality is "external," that "experience" is an "interaction" between the subjective human organism and his "objective environment." What seems to obscure the truth of the constructive workableness of self trust and self credit is the illusion that there *can* be some basis of human meaningfulness other than one's own self activity.

There are not two realities, one internal the other "external," for me to choose from. e.g., my individuality and the rest of the world. There are two choices I can make, namely, acknowledge I am all that I live or deny that certainty. My every life experience is carried as either a conscious self credit or conscious self debit account, depending upon whether I consciously enrich or impoverish my admitted self possession with it. My *only* alternative to observing my life as my own (including my all as my life's dynamic creation) is to overlook the intactness of my own individuality.

My point cannot be made too often or too specifically: I have no choice to *be* other than myself, but I can choose to disregard that necessity. All of my phantom problems of phantasied plurality derive from my necessity to help myself by concentrating upon whatever of my living I *can* integrate with love, at the expense of withholding my appreciation for my personal identity from my too unhappy self experiences.

This resort to apparent mental division obscures the oneness of my oneness, and sets up appearance of plurality where there is only the individuality of my individuality. My every scheme involving the illusion of more-than-one (or of less-than-one) depends upon my mind's capacity to imagine its primary schism: I and not-I. Good examples are opposites such as: internal-external, subjective-objective, idealism-materialism, god-devil, health-sickness, right-wrong, perfect-imperfect, and on and on. The truth is that each so-called opposite develops all of its meaning in terms of *its* so-called opposite. Hot develops all of its meaning from its cold; virtue develops all of its meaning from its vice; wise from its foolish; not-I from its I; altruism from its selfishness; love from its hate; well from its ill; and on and on. Every negation consists only of existence which is negated.

The individual simply *cannot* refuse to accept his responsibility for possessing and directing his own life, but he can appear to himself to be able to do so. I absolutely *cannot* live selflessly or unselfishly or objectively or impersonally or relatively, or other than absolutely individually. But I can believe that I can, or imagine that I can. And this possibility (that I can *seem* to myself to be able to get out of myself, or get somebody or something into myself) is all that can require my immeasurable difficulty called "mental trouble." *My psychotherapy is my learning how to use my mind so that its diremptive power will not obscure or alter my persevering consciousness for the reality of my unremitting oneness.*

However this one and only unit of mental health (one's own acknowledgeable mental activity) is too difficult to be appreciated as indispensable by one of "the majority of the people." Indeed my every kind of individual educational venture dependent upon "the majority of the people" for its success (newspaper, book, journal, T-V program, lecture, all of the other "mass media of communication") *regularly* ignores the force of self insightfulness. *Although little or nothing may be made over this ever so costly self disregard, nevertheless all that passes for "mental disorder" is traceable directly to it.*

I find any definition of health mindedness which does not concentrate and elaborate upon individual mind consciousness as its integrating force simply misses the heart and soul of the matter. It seems evident that "life mindedness" is the product only of work in one's clearly observable introspective field. Only opportunities I make for my self to appreciate my concrete individuality's allness *can* educate me to expertness in this rewarding way of life. The limited regard I was able to pay to my infant dignity and its unquestioned wholeness and allness hardly awakened me to the truth of my unique individuality. I earn conscious vitality from my study of these earliest mental events ignoring my meaning for my personal identity. Individuality is the only affirmation of all affirmations, hence the importance of *conscious* individuality. Restoring my appreciation for the rightness, helpfulness, instructiveness, of *all* of my life experience is my full awakening of and to my self.

"Normality," to the extent that it is judged to be a statistical concept or the acceptable behavior of "the majority of the people," is used by each individual as unrecognized resistance against his developing the comprehensive view of the real fullness, wholeness and intactness of his wonderful creaturehood. My everyone's conception of "normal mentality" is of most profound meaning for the way in which he conducts his life,—and that is a truth of such far-reaching consequence that it merits closest hold. Most important movements of my mind are subject to directions and levels of my willing devotion.

To illustrate, I tend to feel hurt or insecure or confident or whatever, just according to my need for such feeling, not according to any other factual indications. No matter what my over-looked facts are regarding my accepted view of "normality," I need to feel assured that it is the right view also on account of its being mine, so that I can feel confident that I am all right. My attitude that I am already possessed of the most helpful definition of "normality" may operate against my taking the trouble to find out just how inadequate that definition really may be. My fellowman, functioning similarly, settles for a sta-tistical concept of "normality," finding confirmation for its practicality in seeing his fellowman support it. Thus each one may allow the apparent agreeableness of his behavior to do ser-vice for the adequacy of it, thereby forfeiting access to his store of spiritual (subjectively appreciated) potency.

It is urgently essential that the right meaning for such an apparently authoritative term as "normality" be promptly worked up. Any statistical accounting for the definition of such a meaningful concept absolutely rules out full accuracy. The only possible source of accuracy for such definition must be in terms of the given individual mind only. *Whenever careful study of the facts concerning an individual mind is made, the resulting finding is that these facts always perfectly justify the nature and needs of that mind and sufficiently explicate the conduct of that mind.* Work in terms of the individual only, always reveals his mind to be "normally" developed, "normally" healthful, and "normally" functioning. Certainly such self knowledge re-garding the basic nature of his lawbreaker is essential for every governmental officer, beginning with the peacemaking policeman.

Obviously this fact-finding rules out completely the faultfind-ing based upon conclusions arrived at without sufficient relevant facts. Less obviously, this fact-finding cannot be undertaken by "the majority of the people" (rightly described as an abstraction in the mind of the given individual making it up). Pitirim Sorokin refers to a "particular" conception of God as being nothing but the hypostatized *society* of the people. This view calls attention to the extreme degree an individual's very own created conception can appear to him to exert "foreign" power over him. Thus it is with all of my very own insightless living of my self experience (self activity which I cannot observe is my own, but must classify as "not-I"). All such "not-I" living of mine develops powerfully so that I cannot but acknowledge its force, even though I cannot claim it as my own along with the rest of my recognized personal identity.

Reading my Thomas Paine frequently turns out be an exercise in clear observation of political theory:

> Almost everything appertaining to the circumstances of a nation has been absorbed and confounded under the general and mysterious word government. Though it avoids taking to its account the errors it commits and the mischiefs it occasions, it fails not to arrogate to itself whatever has the appearance of prosperity. It robs industry of its honors by pedantically making itself the cause of its effects; and purloins from the general character of man the merits that appertain to him as a social being.

Keenly conscious self sovereignty is the only kind of human control compatible either with cherished sanity or morality or civic mindedness. In order for my mental act to be a sane one, it must be clearly recognizable by me as *my* mental act. In order for my conduct to be moral it must be voluntarily willed by me as my own choice of action. In order for my political action to be democratic it must be acknowledgeable by me as my volitional self control disciplining my self to be able to appreciate and enjoy my individual freedom. To be sure I deal only in so-called "metaphysical" ideas but then only metaphysical ideas belong in the scientific domain of the demonstrable, namely, self observation: man's one possibility for continuing enjoyment of his internal functioning of his absolute essence.

I deem it patriotic to see my democratic government as all and only my own, and my "majority of the people" as nothing but a function of my own mind for preserving my *recognizable* self sovereignty. Alexander Hamilton observed, "Your people, sir—Your people is a great *beast*." I am my "People." Social scientist and psychologist Lawrence K. Frank saw his American view:

> The ancient dichotomy of the individual and society will sooner or later be dissolved as we understand that society is in each individual

and what we call "social adjustment" is essentially the individual's relation to himself.

Individuality is ubiquitous throughout my world. Sense, perceive, feel, observe, or experience whatever I will, in any way possible,—all I can discover is individuality. Whatever entity I consider, is constituted of individuality. To be is to be individual. Every possible is an individual possible. This oneness-orientation is not prudently to be taken for granted by me but rather is wisely to be featured as the *sanity aspect* of human experience, for it is the true form of all that can be meant by my term "reality." Thus I find it both futile and foolhardy to appeal for support to any imaginable source of helpfulness beyond my individual being, my being individuality.

The making of an American citizen is a private, subjective, individualistic creation, evolving through his heeded self experience. Thus Gertrude Stein characteristically looked hard at her making her self, minding "What made me myself inside me." She originally exalted the conscious individualizing nature of her American way of life, appreciating the helpfulness of "an orderly history of everyone who ever was or is or will be living." This responsible conduct of a human life is ever the greatest human achievement, and likewise the hardest. President John F. Kennedy put it pithily, Peace and Freedom are not cheap to come by.

Many an educator has grappled seriously and effectively with his all-important American citizen concern: the urgent continuing need for each individual's purposefully disciplining his mind with and for the privileges and controls of his "democracy." If I stop to heed the great mental discipline required even to be able to tolerate the mental tension excited by this topic statement, I must take heart before proceeding.

Any "learning" which does not result in the student's intentionally advancing his self appreciation, is best described as discipline in and for ignorance about his life's real meaning. His "life's real meaning" consists of his growing recognition of his very own self world as being *his* only world. His discovering this comprehensive view of his individuality also enables him to realize that his every fellowman (wittingly or unwittingly) creates that one's only self world.

Exactly when I use my mind with the insight that it is all and only mine and about me can I consider myself a consciously "free" man. Liberty's joy cannot be inherited or donated. It is worked up in exactly the same way that all mental health is, namely, by assuming the austerities of self confrontation (by my paying profound and steady heed to the single fact that it is my life only that creates all of my every experience). In my opinion, my greatest national urgency is for my every citizen's recognition of his dire neglect of the fact that his American education is: *continuously heeded self education*. This specific civic responsibility of mine is fully as critical now as at the founding of my Republic or during my Civil War period.

Major articles of democratic wisdom, of an American's awakening to his self, may be set down as each self educator's insightfully realizing: every human being is "created equal" to his self; every person is political, in possessing the ingredients in his human nature for gradually working up his self control; each citizen can learn how he can conceive his everyone (*his* "society") as his own self functioning; the fundamental purpose of his education, formal or informal, is the enhancement of his awareness of his self as a world of a person rather than a person of the world; his greatest liberty is that of realizing that his liberty's real meaning is most difficultly learned; his perserveringly observing that the "State" exists for individual man, not individual man for the "State;" *his* "Country" derives all of its importance from his own unique personal living of that meaning; he becomes what he experiences (all of his knowledge is self knowledge, and none of his knowing is foreign to him); the spirited and inspiriting strengths of independence, competence, self reliance, hardihood, integrity, generosity, perseverance, initiative, creativity, imagination, understanding, peace, ethical and esthetic pleasures of subjectivity, and similar self devotions, are developed only to the extent that the pupil can grow to realize that his school (its structure, teacher, fellow pupil, and all) exists only in him, not he in "the" school.

Awakening to American citizenship is self discipline of a very special order whereby the student finds: everything that happens, important or unimportant, happens *entirely within him;* he is not a "unit of society," and also all that he can possibly mean by "society" is united in him; only conscious self study *can* serve education for freedom; his proper self study is to liberate his mind from all enslavement to self ignoration and self neglect; his knowledge is strictly and only his learning about his own magnanimity; only experience clearly recognizable as self experience creates his awakened mind; every claim that "fighting the opposition," "making war upon the enemy," "punishing the transgressor," or any such reliance upon force (other than the power of love) to "win the peace," is based upon insufficient facts; all of his "civil disobedience" is self relevant only; peaceful procedure is his safe and sane method for developing his new policy of any kind.

In his thoughtful essay, *The Origins Of The American Mind,* self sensible Lewis Mumford describes how unconscious use of abstraction can serve to conceal one's own process of thinking, so that his use of his mind appears to lose its real meaning as being only and entirely a succession of his own organic experiences, for all of which he is completely responsible. Mumford sees how his abstraction must seem to be "externalized," once it is not evident as his own *internality.* The abstraction "human individuality" is always the living creation of the person who conceives it and, as such, it must refer only to that person. My unconscious habit of trying to make it refer to "somebody else," if successful, would deprive it of its only humanity, my own, and drive me "out of my mind." A meaning without a biological basis, is impossible, and my every so-called "externalization" of my abstraction merely reveals my unreadiness to claim it as my own.

I observe that the preservation of my legalized self sovereignty is seriously threatened by desperations based upon insightless views of such meaningful abstractions as "freedom," "civil rights," "equality," "democracy." Such extremes of human endurance, traceable to unpreparedness for recognizable self sovereignty, may or may not exceed the understanding or toleration of my governmental representative.

My personal experience has sensitized me to the immense safety I find in my conscious, *individuality respecting and indiscriminating* self sovereignty, and to the enormous danger I see in my unconscious, *individuality ignoring or discriminating* "State" sovereignty. The hindsight I developed from that living I would now convert to foresight. In 1781 Jefferson wrote, "An elective despotism is not the government we fought for."

During 1935, 1936 and 1937, while residing in Vienna, I watched the rapid rising of my fellowman's Nazi Germany, his swiftly moving shift of loyalty to his State from his recognizable personal identity, his desperate effort to try to arouse his self further to the imminent dangers of dictatorship,—and such a death dealing kind of despotism! I viewed my young Nazi radical, oh so eager to overthrow his "established" policy, and oh so reckless as to what government of self intolerance he must then offer in its place. Even more painfully, I observed many an immediate and dear friend difficultly awakening to the likelihood that either his avoiding or enduring the nearly incredible estrangement of his very own countryman self maddened by his "Hitler youth movement," must cost his life.

To be something of a self alarmist is my intention in setting forth the tremendous benefit I have derived from awakening to my comprehensive view of my individuality, as well as the enormous life risks I have run from sparing my somnolence for my self's allness. *It is too rare for me to be able right now to find my American fellow citizen who is ready to declare that his government is his own, that his State exists for and in him, that his Society is his self creation, that there can be no real difference between his private principle and his public practice.* Furthermore, I believe my senses in observing that such ignorance of civic fact speaks for its self in inviting the over-extension of control unrecognizable as self government. My ever so promising down-hill course from my decentralized to my centralized governmental power now places the heaviest possible strain upon my mind's capacity to see such concentration of governmental authority as compatible with conscious citizen sovereignty. Enormous and ever increasing inflation can no longer be denied. Even its suicidal significance as a political weapon seems incomprehensible. I know I must either wake up to acknowledged responsibility for my being *my* individuality-revering government in dire danger of dissolution, or suffer the consequence of some illusion of "external" dictatorship.

With my Emerson, I often shudder when I take the trouble to realize that my God is a just God. In his *Emerson In Suburbia* writes Samuel Withers, Administrative Director of the Council for Basic Education, "But Emerson does not go over in today's suburbia. The boys and girls whom I taught English in a wealthy New York suburb . . . just can't dig Emerson . . . are suspicious of this self-trust . . . 'What I must do is all that concerns me,' Emerson said, 'not what the people think' . . . my qualms are about tomorrows leaders . . . We need, ourselves, to believe in the sacredness of the integrity of our own minds . . . Stoutheartedness, engenders stoutheartedness."

But stoutheartedness, never the product of spontaneous combustion, is always the creation of conscious self appreciation, of honored human individuality. My self reliance cannot result from dependence upon anyone but my own acknowledged self. If I cannot believe in my own marvelous power I have no possibility other than to believe in the use of some force I cannot recognize as my own but vaguely refer to as "the government." Just then the termination of my devotion to a "government of the free man" has its forceful beginning. If I ever have realized that "government" can do nothing and that all that is creative or productive is the issue of human individuality, I either overlook the fact entirely or vaguely assume that my "government man" can adequately take the place of my conscious self government. Right here the point needs making that no other promising "leadership" can possibly help me, since my only real helpfulness must come from my conscious *self* leadership. No one else can lead my life. I have observed the futility inherent in the Fuhrer's efforts to govern everyone but his self.

In *The Philosophy of Physical Science,* Sir Arthur Eddington helpfully italicized, *it is actually an aid in the search for knowledge to understand the nature of the knowledge which we seek.* I help my self as a student to be realizing that the nature of the knowledge I seek is thoroughly my own human nature.

My developing long-sighted views of my self benefit depends
entirely upon my willingness to undergo my painfully difficult
processes of my conscious self awakening. As noted, this my-
living-is-my-learning self discipline, essential for the American
citizen's training his mind, cannot be secured from any formal
schooling that I can discover. I secure from the purely well-
intentioned reporting of my American Council of Learned
Societies, or my Commission on Liberal Education, and so on,
what I expect from it after soberly considering its title: seemingly unconscious personification, pluralization, and pejoration
or melioration. To illustrate, without any intention of faultfind-
ing, "Our academic 'humanists' must make a resolute effort to
reorient themselves, to clarify their own objectives and to
provide the academic community with a type of guidance which
reflects genuine comprehension of basic issues," or, "Many
humanistic faculties have lost their way and forfeited public
confidence." or, "Education has a double function—to make
men free and to teach them to bear freedom when they have it,"
or, "No one believes in solipsism, and very few now even assert
that they do."

The only possible, hence safe and sane, centralism is in each
citizen's own acknowledged being. Dean Russell of the Foundation for Economic Education poses profoundly meaningful
questioning, "Do you know of any action now being performed
by government that would be illegitimate and immoral for you
to do as an individual? If so, here is a disturbing question: What
is the source of the government's authority to perform that
action?" I say to my self, "My American government must not
be a greatly watered down version of reverence for human individuality." John Stuart Mill worded the consequence of such a
possibility, "A state which dwarfs its men, in order that they
may be more docile instruments in its hands—even for beneficial purposes—will find that with small men no great thing can
really be accomplished." In 1962 Maurice H. Stans addresses
his United States Chamber of Commerce members thus, "We
are gradually surrendering our American spirit, based on initiative and self-reliance, for a social and economic mess of pottage.
. . . . Our fiscal policies are an open invitation to a crisis for the
dollar."

My conscious self education is *all* with which I can help my self to become the responsible citizen I need to become. All of my American government is helpfully observable as my personification of my right and privilege to my individual vote. My educating myself to that citizen comprehension occurred when I orginated it along with other precious civic wisdom, from my observing each member of my family creating it consciously for his own self appreciation.*

Now earnest but premature questioning arises. Yes, but how am I going to change "the established system"? How am I going to start a "Do it yourself for yourself" plan of education? How can I, one person, make over or even find fault with my dearly achieved and established public school development? Such inquiry affords opportunity for me to heed that none of my observation is intended as finding fault. Rather, it merely calls my attention to the wonderful resourcefulness and resiliency of my individual human nature. How basically helpful it is that my human constitution demands either that its nature and needs be heeded, or it indicates immediately with painfully revealing signs and symptoms that one or another of its vitally important prerequisites is being disregarded!

Nineteenth century French political scientist Frederic Bastiat** quite as did his fellow citizen Destutt de Tracy before him, could regard the making of his ideal citizenship in terms of the most orderly expression of his human constitution: "Life, liberty, and property do not exist because men have made laws. On the contrary, it was the fact that life, liberty, and property existed beforehand that caused men to make laws in the first place." And, "See if the law benefits one citizen at the expense of another by doing what the citizen himself cannot do without committing a crime."

It is understandable that the patient do all of the complaining. He is doing the suffering with little or no recognition of the facts fully accounting for the functioning of his distress, with little or no understanding of the lifesaving value of his present need to

*See Index, Dorsey.
***The Law,* Irvington, New York, Foundation for Economic Education.

"find fault." His physician's diagnosis however need have no faultfinding in it. Rightly it contains praise for the perfect working for good of all of the facts involved in his patient's condition.

The issue at stake is not yet, How to change my American schooling. That will come later, only after the lesson is fully learned about what my *present* American education does, and properly must do, as long as it continues in force. *My present American education is accomplishing exactly what it should accomplish rather than only what my patriotic hopes or expectations wish from it.*

It is a boon to discover how my own created illusion of learning about an impersonal objective external world disciplines my mind in esteeming this illusion at the expense of my appreciation for its creator. But it is a startling experience that teaches me consciously to develop my own mental power *as* my own, quite as I do my own cultivation of my power I call "physical." My so-called "objectivity" cannot be anything but a hiding place for my subjectivity. There being no experience but self experience, I can learn only from that personal realm.

The chief symptom of my obstructed awareness for my self, is my addiction to my resulting phantom problems: What does my fellowman think of me? What is my fellowman saying or doing or maybe even plotting about me? How can I get someone else to pay attention to my needs? Similar questioning indicates my own need to live my self heedfully.

Inquiry into the nature of my human freedom properly concerns itself with my liberating my self about my early established mental habits. As a child I imagine that my wonderful capacity to be self conscious can be somehow displaced, so that it certainly seems possible some one else can be conscious of me. If I do not recognize the entirety of my own itegration, but rather seem to myself to be made up of separate parts, some of which I cannot even recognize as my very own,—then I cannot see that my wholeness is intact, but rather seem to see "separation" everywhere. Then I must look at my world only as if it is "outside" of me, comprised of innumerable beings or things which I seem to be able to view "from the outside," but only *from the outside.* I may even tend to overlook the obvious truth that each being or thing is composed only of its wholly *internal* self, and not of anything "external" to it. I cannot realize that my asserted view of "it" apparently "from the outside of it," can have nothing whatsoever to do with any living but my own.

If I use my mind *insightfully,* that is, use it and at the same time realize that I *am* using it, then I succeed to a right view of its integration. Everybody and everything being absolutely nothing but itself, it is thereby describable as completely integrated. Whatever is, is all its self. Its every possible meaning is all and only meaningful for its self. Thus, if I a white say or think something I consider to be about "a black," all I can really be saying or thinking must be entirely about my self, about my very own experiences that I name "a black." Being a black, all I can mean by "a white" is special living of my very own that I have named "a white."

"A white can never know what it is to be black." Certainly not. No one person can ever know what it is to be another person. A black can never know what it is to be any other black. A white can never know what it is to be any other white. A white *can* know what it is to be *his* other black or *his* other white. A black *can* know what it is to be *his* other white or *his* other black.

All of the phantom problems created by my illusion of "segregation" are dispelled by my realizing the truth of my unsegregatable wholeness, my inviolable integration as an intact individual. Above all, it is critically important for me to discover what it means to be my complete self. I appreciate my greatness entirely to the extent of my freedom to use my mind consciously to observe: my functioning power I cannot claim, is my only possible "invisible" government.

I am not partial to being designated by any special characteristic such as my color. I do not enjoy being called "white" or "black" or "yellow" or "red," for purpose of being "classified" somehow. I am in a class by my self. Quite apart from the obvious disadvantage in any such contemptuous name-calling of my self as "pale face" or "red skin," it seems defensible to wish to be nominated only as being the *whole* human individual I actually am.

As American citizen I voluntarily subjugate my self to literally *millions* of my American government's laws, each one of them in turn liable to my right to dissent. I recognize that I subserve innumerable laws of my human constitution as well, merely by my preferring to obey them and live, rather than ignore them and die. The more I turn from this helpful self perspective, the more I turn to fatal self disobedience.

I cannot extend my conscious self tolerance to include my very own living I associate with dislike, *unless I can see and appreciate my life's good working itself up in this generous view of my personal identity.* My learning thus to "see" and "appreciate" more of the real extent of my individuality, is a process of *conscious self education* only. "Somebody else" cannot tell it to me, nor can I learn it from "somebody else." However, I must experience this lifesaving conscious self development or pay the consequence in symptom development, such as heedlessness for my best interests in the name of harm to "someone else." *My sign or symptom forms whenever my self awareness cannot function freely.* When I cannot express my self so that I can recognize my self in the expression then I can no longer *feel* my responsibility for my behavior. Thus I may become violent "towards my fellowman" without realizing I am harming my self thereby.

Although awakening to the fact that *all* violence is self violence is a desirable reality for everyone, it is a specifically desirable realization for anyone who would seek to represent his fellowman officially. Inestimable distress can be traced directly to the insightless "representative of the people." Every citizen's democratic way of life requires therefore a representative of a specific type of personality, *an individual who has made his self the possesor of emotional self continence.* Where a so-called representative lacks self vision, his "people" in the form of each individual he "represents" must suffer accordingly. Self vision or self violence is the law of human individuality. Therefore some explication of the free and brave functioning of human violence is in order. Aristotle clarified, "He should know how to govern like a free man, and how to obey like a free man."

My ideal nonviolence consists of my living all of my violent thoughts, feelings and actions *continently,* that is, within the range of my conscious mind, thus realizing that each violence is relevant to my self only. Certainly this ability to endure my most distressing ideas and emotions with composure, and to be able to consider myself as acting upon them, by using my creative imagination consciously for that purpose,—surely this is clearly an accomplishment only of a mind disciplined specifically with freedom's force, *self consciousness.*

I am born able to be violent, but I must labor hard to be able to control my self. Self discipline is not easy. Pericles noticed: "We live at ease, not like the Lacedaemonians who undergo laborious exercises to be brave." Obviously my achievement of continence with regard to my capacities for violence is the consequence of my most reluctant, yet most desirable, awakening to emotional control. Only this specific self control can spare me nightmarish experiences of thinking that my ravings and ragings can affect somebody else, or that somebody else's ravings and ragings can affect me. Thus, "He makes me angry," or "I can't stand him," or "I hate her," or "He is afraid of me," or "I'll get even with him," or "I am jealous of her,"—each such observation reveals emotional incontinence based upon lack of self insight. Self insight would reveal, "He" as *my He,* "him" as *my him,* "her" as *my her,* and so on.

My extending my awareness for my individuality by awakening to its factuality has resulted not only in my strengthening my conscious will power but also in my relieving my self of the corresponding amount of involuntary behavior. Similarly my practicing arousal of my self to my self has enabled me to study the marvelous helpfulness in the rich abundance of my emotionality. Now nothing appears more beneficial to me than the certainty with which I may discipline my mind to govern, rather than seem governed by, the strong feelings essential for my sensing the meaningfulness of my living.

My so-called violence is my natural resort to a form of emotional helpfulness that worked well for me during my early years of development. By expressing my nature and needs "violently" I then succeeded in securing the comfort and care I needed for staying alive. Gradually I awakened to my self sufficiently to be able to renounce much of this *unrecognizable* self helpfulness in favor of *appreciated* self helpfulness. However, with every seeming breakdown of the latter I tend to resort to a breakthrough of the former. *My working up my understanding of my every unhappy feeling as a signal that my conscious self possession is momentarily at stake, has been my most sanatory life lesson.*

N. Katkov observed, "Having ideas in one's head which can never be applied is a torture, a terrible torture." The *being* of such an idea is its tormenting application, I find. I cannot "have" an idea, I must *be* it. Similarly, I cannot "have" an emotion, I must *be* it, and be all that I live as associated with it. *My capacity for living every kind of emotion as my own understandable biological functioning is what gives my life its precious variety as well as its strong feeling of reality.*

And now to the lifesaving importance of conscious emotional control for my American government! Emotional pains such as anger, rage, hatred, fear, and so on, are standard human equipment. Everyone must live such mental hurts, either consciously or unconsciously, either in a self "contained" or self "overwhelmed" way. The citizen who has disciplined his mind with *self* responsibility is imaginative in peacemaking. The citizen who has disciplined his mind to regard his fellowman as other than self responsible is imaginative in war making!

I can point only in one and the same direction, selfward, for designating anything and everything about all of my world, including my feelings. Only *I* am the hating, the hater, and the hated. Only *I* am the fearing, the fearful, and the feared. Whatever the emotion, *I* am the only sentient one who feels, *I* am the only sapient one who feels with awareness, *I* am the only sleeping one who feels with unawareness.

Only my knowledge that is thoroughly effective in my behavior is thoroughly entitled to the name. A clear illustration of *knowing* what is happening, is a mother's sensing her own unbearable discomfort in hearing her infant's cry. Actually knowing that my fellowman is entirely my own living of all that I mean by "my fellowman" is my most valuable insight for helping me to "represent" either *my* "friend" or *my* "opponent" with the least self hurt.

Although my Kerner report (my abridged U. S. Riot Commission Report) contains reference to human individuality, it understandably orients itself largely as follows:

> The record before this Commission reveals that the causes of recent racial disorders are imbedded in a massive tangle of issues and circumstances—social, economic, political, and psychological—which arise out of the historical pattern of Negro-white relations in America.

In due detail the report illustrates the force of individual helpfulness also by recording Booker T. Washington's insightful view of toilsome self development for life appreciation:

> "Self-help and self-respect appeared a practical and sure, if gradual, way of ultimately achieving racial equality. Washington's doctrines also gained support because they appealed to race pride—if Negroes believed in themselves, stood together, and supported each other, they would be able to shape their destinies."

I remind my self of Plato's philosophy of steadfast devotion "to those things in which God abides and in beholding which" the mind conscious one "is what he is."

The joy of living to be derived from the steady consciousness of self fulfillment is second to none. Heeding that my every experience is fulfilling my nature is my surest source of life satisfaction. In every other way of life I discover the helpful signs and symptoms of my dangerous obscuration of my consciousness for its one and only biologically adequate subject, namely, my pure selfhood.

It is never possible to suffer any limitation of my only activity, self activity, but it is readily possible to endure self unawareness until custom makes it even comfortable. My realization that my conscious responsibility is surely the only possible force that *can* awaken me to my costly habit of "taking my self for granted" or otherwise dulling my appreciation for the wholeness, oneness, and allness of my self, is my most ideal and practical realization. Once it comes alive in my consciousness, I know finally what "becoming an adult citizen with an adult citizen's responsibility" really means. I know also just what my Abraham Lincoln meant when he proclaimed,*

> Of our political revolution of '76 we all are justly proud. It has given us a degree of political freedom far exceeding that of any other of the nations of the earth. In it the world has found a solution of that long mooted problem as to the capability of man to govern himself. . . . Happy day, when, all appetites controlled, all passions subdued, all matters subjected, mind, all-conquering mind, shall live and move, the monarch of the world. Glorious consummation! Hail fall of Fury! Reign of Reason, all hail!

Lincoln's phrase, "all matters subjected," can scarcely be lived comfortably by any fellow scientist of mine whose mental habit of (illusional) "objectivity" obscures his biological necessity for total subjectivity. Of his consciously subjective colleague, as of his psychiatric patient, he must resort to some form of self rejection such as, "Nobody can understand him," or "He is a mystic," or the paradoxical "He is out of his mind." In his "Tales of Jacob" insightful Thomas Mann consciously subjectivizes:

> The conception of individuality belongs after all to the same category of conceptions as that of unity and entirety, the whole and the all; and in the days of which I am writing (the ancient biblical times) the distinction between spirit in general and individual spirit possessed not nearly so much power over the mind as in our world of to-day. . . . It is highly significant that in those days there were no words for conceptions dealing with personality and individuality.

My current self experience of a workshop in race relations effectively demonstrated the vital importance in my disciplining my mind to awaken to the helpfulness in *every* thought that might "occur" to it, by willingly seeing my precious personal identity in any of my thinking, instead of losing my "presence of mind" in overwhelming excitement "about it." I had been kindly advised that the session would be a most difficult occasion, because of flaring tempers, glaring inconsistencies, and

*Address to Springfield Washington Temperance Society, 1842.

bewildering ideas. Certainly in this kind of workshop "trouble-some," "controversial" and similarly "difficult" thoughts are in great demand.

By beginning with voiced statements to my self about 1) acknowledgeable individual responsibility, 2) a special wish that each worker be willing to introduce his private views by mentioning his name, and 3) the fact that I was and would be seeing my personal identity in every individual of my workshop, I promptly succeeded in advancing sober consideration as a worthy mental goal. Next, I described how I must either try to see the good workableness in my *every* thought, however unpleasant or even hateful it might appear at first, or else disqualify myself temporarily from being able to work properly with that thought. I pointed out that "race" is ONLY a name for a meaning *in an individual mind,* and that "relations" is ONLY a name for associations *within an individual mind.* With this kind of *self contained* orientation, each worker then proceeded earnestly and without any untoward commotion or self belittlement.

In his wholesomely refreshing study "Who Do You Think You Are,"* lifeward author Roy P. Basler observes, "The quest for identity has been the theme of American literature from James Fenimore Cooper to William Faulkner. All of our great writers have told one story—of men, and women too, seeking to learn who they are, and in the performance of the quest finding out and showing who they are—creating their identity out of the stuff of life itself."

I, including everyone of *my* world, might well say to my self; "Regularly taking my self for granted, rather than being constantly amazed at my wonderful nature, is to lack understanding for the marvelous one I am. I may trace all of my life's dissatisfaction to my overlooking my true greatness and goodness. I have never actually examined what it really means to be my self at all comprehensively, and what I have not taken the trouble to observe about my nature is what must trouble me mostly until I do. Certainly I have helped my self, particularly to avoid over-

*Midway, University of Chicago Press, Vol. 8, No. 2, 1967

powering exertion, by not claiming all of my living as being my own. However the fact is that *I am all of my life* and the cost in my disowning any of it is enormous in terms of my duly appreciating my completeness."

My present hard earned realization that I must continue arduously to search out the laws of my human constitution and discipline my self to honor each one of them, is my most helpful insight for enlarging my acknowledgable personal identity to correspond with my constant self growth.

Thomas Jefferson

REPRESENTATIVE GOVERNMENT

"No popularity lives long in a democracy."
John Quincy Adams

"Representative government" is each mind's meaning, indicating that every elector creates his representative as an entity of his own life, and that each representative creates each of his electors (as an entity of his own creaturehood). Human being cannot be delegated or represented out of itself. A mature democratic "leader" recognizes that each of his supporters lives his own leader. *A leader is made up of leadership, not of followership.* There is no aspect of my living that I cannot personify and therefore it is my identity-honoring responsibility to heed my every personification.

The only authority in my government-by-representation is not the will of my representative but rather the will I put into my own vote. Only conscious self rule can be vitalizing for the ruler. My practicing the doctrine of nonidentity, the negation of being, pronounces the doom of my democracy.

No less a price than my awakening to my full identity must be paid for my building my world according to my ideal specifications issuing under the constitutional law of my own growth. My realizing that *I* create my experience constitutes my living it freely. The question of my freedom finds its answer in the limits of my acknowledged individuality, of my revering my growing being. I note with self-satisfaction how often I use self conscious words such as "I," "my," "only," "entirely," "wholly," and the like. "I am the State," said Louis XIV and Napoleon. How different the course of history had either one said, "I am my State."

His democracy enables every citizen to declare that he is his own representative, that his agent or deputy or substitute consists entirely of his own psychic living. The full-grown (worldwide) American sees clearly that one individual cannot bear the authority or character of another. The consciously self

45

possessed American does not confound his imaginings of representation with illusional externality. Democracy means, "I am equal to me," and "My representative is equal to his self." Self possession rules out foreign representation. "It is hard for an empty sack to stand upright," said Benjamin Franklin.

My abstraction or personification such as "representative government," "arm of the law," "political force," or "social idealism," is a fine toboggan for my sliding out of my right mind so that I can devote myself painlessly to my personal living of self hurt, become "hellbent on doing good," and create the various crazes of the fanaticism motivated by my repudiated individuality. I may make every kind of a self deceiver of myself as long as I comfort myself with my illusion that I have many others "on my side." My realizing my absolute individuality clarifies my necessity for the prudence which my sense of my true oneness enforces. I cannot take my "everything" into account in framing my peace plan (unified world) unless I can take my "everyone and everything" into account as being mine. My real unity affirms itself in and through its apparent diversity. Seeing all of my "represented" and "representative" world as my own, I sense that I cannot afford to be anesthetic about it. Alexander Pope integrated his mind consciously with many an insight:

> Thus God and Nature formed the general frame,
> And bade self-love and social be the same.

It is my fundamental privilege consciously to own my "representative" as my self property. My right to my self property is the basis of my every other right or responsibility, and cannot be well ignored by me. I tax myself most heavily "without representation" for my devotion to remaining self unconscious. Insofar as I am self unconscious, my sovereignty as an individual must seem to me at best a kind of romantic notion. My disclaimer of any intent to live me as my self, cannot in any sense prevent it. In my awakening of my full consciousness, namely, my self awareness, I enable my self to look all around in the world of my self and thus look over vital resources I must otherwise overlook.

My ideal of self government is only as strong as I make it. I can take liberties with my own self property. I cannot take liberties with the self property of my fellowman. Only (my) he can do that. My living of my appreciation for my full autonomy enforces my seeing my fellowman's full autonomy. My appreciation for *my* fellowman "grows upon aquaintance." Asking my self, What kind of self orientation do I find most helpful?, my reply is implicit in my question. Certainly my appreciation for the meaning of my intact wholeness is my most helpful self understanding. My observing my truth enables me to be conscious for my wholeness, and also my realization of my wholeness subsumes my every other realization.

This I conceive to be my American ideal: My right to, and responsibility for, my fullest conscious self development. My "public virtue" is entirely a matter of my private virtue. With every access of self consciousness I regnerate and revitalize my democratic way of life. Not by ancestor worship, not by the worship of god whom I refuse to see as my own, but by the worship of my all as my own soul, do I get a glimpse of the heroic view of what it means to be human. It is comforting to realize that I shall always want excellence until my mind's eye works hard enough to see that I already am it. Henry Ford also invented this economical view: "Life is work, and everything you do is so much experience. . . . What does anyone make but a living? And whatever you have, you must either use or lose."

It is necessary to choose between realistic self satisfaction and illusional "popularity," between solid self esteem and ephemeral fame. To the extent that I depend upon the opinion of my fellowman for my appreciation of my self worth, I must not have access to my conscious self respect. 1952, in Detroit, Adlai E. Stevenson, speaking on Safeguards against Communism, said, "My definition of a free society is a society where it is safe to be unpopular. I want to keep our America that way."

Andrew Jackson

MY AMERICAN UNION

"But I wish to be distinctly understood on one point. Americanism is a question of spirit, convictions and purpose, not of creed or birthplace."

Theodore Roosevelt

My ancient wise man placed the golden age of united mankind in the past. My modern man of science tends to place that golden age of unified humanity in the future. The only possible human age, of any description, is the present. And as George Santayana declared, Individualism is "the only ideal possible," also, "It was Locke who first thought of looking into his own breast to find there the genuine properties of gold and of an apple; and it is clear that nothing but lack of consecutiveness and courage kept him from finding the whole universe in the same generous receptacle." The idea of human "progress" as an historic development involves the tempting illusion "comparison," and tends to obscure the view of existing human excellence. There can be no conscious unanimity for me except that achieved by my own creative imagination.

The claim is sometimes made that the best critic, or observer, of American democracy might be an "outsider," one who lives some other government than democracy, a James Bryce or a de Tocqueville. This imagined superiority of an "outsider" must be based upon the self deception that the best observer of an experience is one who has never consciously lived a like experience. It seems to me that *the fully appreciated meaning of self sovereignty can grow itself only where the opportunity for its conscious growth offers.* The sanest traveller finds himself wherever he goes. The self seer travels a great deal, in his life only. My psychology, namely, the condition in which I live my mind, is my only possible source of either my political philosophy or political science. The master principle of my psychology upholds the truth that my mind is all and only about its self, about its own bedrock subjectivity. My conscious growing of my self is entirely my awakening to my potentiality. I consist all and only of monogeneous individuality. *All so-called integration or unifying of my self is merely my daring to wake up fully enough to observe my unity that has always existed.* The wisdom in which my subjectivity, or ideality, or spirit (if you will) finds my joy of living may be worded: I am all and only that I am.

My wholeness, or unity, is the fountain-head of my reality, the source and goal of my being. My growing in the direction of my devotion to my whole, or united, self is my only effectual wide-awake way to extend my self love to include my love for my whole world. My altruism can have no reliable foundation other than in this sincere selfishness of mine. In direct perception of my imaginative insight I find my only possible American, or world, union. My practice of self integration apart from my world is suicidal. Union implies sameness, identity, monogeneity, oneness and allness,—each organic condition indispensable for peace, harmony, or conscious ideality.

The notion that what is ideal and helpful can be somehow imposed on the citizen is one to consider carefully from all sides, for it is "popular," powerful and prevalent. I must live it daily with kindness. It is advanced even as patriotically inspired. The essence of human worth, self love, cannot be drilled into me. My character cannot be formed by so-called "external" influence. My self development is an expression that means what it says: a whole united being discovering his functional power, exploring his potential joy of living, ultimately realizing his personal identity and thereafter viewing his every experience as an adventure in consciously uniting his becoming in his being.

In his book, *America Comes of Age,* André Siegfried described the doctrine of "efficiency in production" as the "central idea" of the American. He asserted, the American "Nation is not individualistic in mentality." He speaks of the American citizen as having become "a means rather than an end." Each of these charges is a grievous one declaring that self consciousness is the desideratum, not the design, of the developed American mind.

The ideal of "service" is healthful to the extent that it is recognizable as self service. A laborer who cannot see his work-a-day world as his own construction within him, suffers from the illusion of insignificantly drudging in an alien and inhuman world. United with his unified fellow creature by the only force which unites, rather than unties, namely, the force of personal identity, a consciously free person observes this union within himself as an act of his own life, an energetic growing self expression. Even "brotherhood" is entirely inadequate to express the true *identity* a man lives when he experiences his fellowman. All that he grows, and most notably *his* fellowman, is a living nisus in his life. Every physician knows that the health importance of self consciousness suffers the most disregard in home, school, or all "social" living, and needs the tenderest care.

Everyone must raise his own ideal of the possibilities of human nature, and he can do that only by discovering that there is more to himself than he formerly supposed. Louis D. Brandeis made the point, "The margin between that which men naturally do, and that which they can do, is so great that a system which urges men on to action and develops individual enterprise and initiative is preferable, in spite of the wastes that necessarily attend that process." *Man's only possible "socialization" is his augmentation of his personal identity,—not the rifling of his individuality.*

Of each man's unific self, no less a student of the human constitution than "world renowned" neurologist Sir Charles Sherrington recorded in his *Man on his Nature,** "Altruism has to grow . . . a soul-growth which shall open out a higher self. . . . The self is the biological pivot of the individual. It amounts to sharing suffering as though another's suffering were its own. . . . Medicine's problem has always had to face the individual. . . . Watching for change within ourselves we note that here our being holds out opportunity. . . . Try then to teach your sight to grow. . . . Altruism as passion, that would seem as yet Nature's noblest product. . . . Mind awakened by distress of mind."

Quite as Thomas Jefferson clearly stated, "Our legislators are not sufficiently apprized of the rightful limits of their power;

*Cambridge, University Press, 1951.

that their true office is to declare and enforce only our natural rights and duties, and to take none of them from us. . . . The idea is quite unfounded, that on entering into society we give up any natural rights. . . . I believe that justice is instinct and innate, that the moral sense is as much a part of our constitution as that of feeling, seeing, or hearing; as a wise creator must have seen to be necessary in an animal destined to live in society; that every human mind feels pleasure in doing good to another.''

Similarly Mencius declared, "To nourish one's nature, is the way to secure heaven. . . . The tendency of man's nature to good, is like the tendency of water to flow downwards.'' The Chinese individual's reverence for *his* past is a chief virtue for his development of wholesome appreciation for the perfection of his being. Confucius said, "An accordance with this nature (man's) is called the Path of Duty.''

LIBERTY

"Among freemen there can be no successful appeal from the ballot to the bullet."

Abraham Lincoln

Another key concept of conscious self government is freedom. George Bernard Shaw to the contrary, American liberty is not just a monstrous idol "put up in New York Harbor." As Lincoln asserted, in giving freedom to the slave we assured freedom to the free. The price of liberty is a specific kind of vigilance, namely, acknowledgeable *self* consciousness.

Scientifically expounded "political science" is presumed to encompass the whole order of modern social organization. All that it can ever possibly be is a set of meanings of an individual mind, psychic elements of the given mind considering it. Any self imperceptive political scientist, however, must limit the word, "individualism," to mean: a social philosophy in political economy. At most, he may courageously concede "primacy," never its allness, to individuality.

Every American can thrill with life by reading the wonderful endorsements by Thomas Jefferson and John Adams of insightful Destutt de Tracy's treatise upon political economy founded upon free appreciation for citizen selfhood. Tracy apparently recognized that the stages of human development of greatest meaning are the stages in the awakening of man's consciousness for his own identity.

My personified "government" cannot grant or withhold the liberty of my free individuality through any extension or limitation of its so-called "political power." In no way can I impair my freedom. Whether I am living my inside or outside of a jail, my liberty (as my individuality) is inviolable.

John Stuart Mill decided, it is "better to be Socrates dissatisfied than a fool satisfied." By sensing fully this truth of my inviolable individuality I can see myself, *de novo*, as ever natural and original, and avoid living myself as if I have a gang or society or an army or any other such phantasm "on my side" to help me. I know that I am selfish about it, but I do enjoy seeing my fellowman look at his autonomous being with similar recognition. Any person who will make the necessary arrangements with himself (as often as possible) for cultivating his own self consciousness, will thus make for his self the strong healthy enjoyable mind characteristic of the ideal United States citizen.

Mental health work and American citizenship training have the same goal: appreciation for human excellence. It is his self consciousness, only, that gives man his unique power of valuing his wonderfulness. His language is a wonderful means for his securing definitive views of his abundance, but has no more "communication" value than has any other self use. Consciousness is mind sight. Dwight Morrow discovered, "As I get older . . . I become more convinced that good government is not a substitute for self-government.

Freedom's only soil is the individual mind. "Servitude" is a state of mind produced by the "master's" repudiating the truth that he is entirely his own "slave." Any of my living which I conduct only as conspicuously mine is obviously "mastered" by me. *Feeling* free only applies to conscious (recognized) freedom; *being* free is the condition of all individuality. Individuality, by definition, is free to be all and only itself. I feel bound by any living of mine which *seems* foreign to me. Conscious self mastery, or unconscious self mystery, is my choice.

Liberty is a quality of subjectivity only and therefore can be felt only where subjectivity is acknowledged. My illusion "objectivity" (as if not-I) is lived by me as if alien to me and as if out of my control. I feel free only when my will *evidently* controls. All that can be meant by becoming an emancipated individual is: becoming conscious about my self freedom which I formerly considered self unfreedom (since I formerly disclaimed identity with some of my will power that was then operative). The feeling of oppression associated with overlooked selfness, derives from the ignored wholeness implicit in disregarded individuality. Freedom's thrill (the appreciation for my intact integrity) is expressed in the satisfying peaceful feeling of innocence.

I cannot awaken my conscious self tolerance to include my

very own living I associate with dislike, *unless I can see and appreciate the benefit to my self in this generous veiw of my personal identity.* I cannot say to my self too often: My learning thus to "see" and "appreciate" more of the real extent of my individuality, is a process of *conscious self education* only. "Somebody else" cannot tell it to me, nor can I learn it from "somebody else." However, I *must* experience this lifesaving conscious self development or pay the consequence in symptom development, such as heedlessness for my best interests in the name of harm to "someone else." My sign or symptom forms whenever my full self awareness cannot function freely. When I cannot express my self so that I can recognize my self in the expression, I can no longer *feel* my responsibility for my behavior. My being violent towards my fellowman without realizing I am harming my self thereby, is analogous to holding my anaesthetized hand in the flame.

I am responsible for the conduct of the world of my self, including all of my "others," whether I have cultivated or ignored my sensitivity for that fact. My denial of my responsibility for any of my living is always at the cost of my enforcing my wholeness-power to maintain whatever recognizable monogeneity I have worked up. Thus, if I deny that I am growing only my self, I necessitate my growing of my living being that I cannot recognize as my self, such as a tumor. To illustrate, my studies indicated clearly to me that I am cancer prone just to the extent that I am prone to disregard my own life's interests in the name of "selfless" devotion to, or dislike for, any "somebody else" or "something else." Most important of all for the present writing is that my resorting to behaving violently towards "somebody else," the "establishment," or whatever, is traceable directly to my shortsighted views of my own self's welfare.

My developing farsighted views of my self benefit depends entirely upon my willingness to undergo the painfully difficult processes of that much acknowledgeable self awakening. At present I see I cannot secure from my formal schooling this consciously self oriented discipline essential for my American citizenship training. Shall I arduously awaken to my responsibility for being all that I can mean by my increasingly vast governmental responsibility? Or, shall I sleepily develop my feelings of guilt, signalling my living my government as if it is external to me? Patriotic Thomas Paine found his fellowman inclined to the latter course. Said he, "Government, like dress, is the badge of lost innocence."

Assuming his duties as Secretary of State, Thomas Jefferson could express doubt whether "the ordinary business of my department will leave me any leisure." Today, State Department personnel number far over twenty thousand. Since 1790 the population of the United States has grown fifty-fold, from 4,000,000 to near 200,000,000. My federal, state and local governments can make my biggest and most meaningful demands upon my power. Hence it is necessary for my appreciating just who I am, to keep track of my self as this expanse. I cannot afford to "lose my mind" in the name of my Country or Government or World. My thought such as "My sun is five billion years old," or "My light travels 186,000 miles per second," or so on, must be appreciated for its only reality as my thought, if I would recognize my infinite and omnipresent subjectivity. In *The Gentle Reader,* wide awake American Samuel Crothers records:

> The border-land between Psychology and Sociology is the scene of many a foray. The Psychologist thinks nothing of following a fleeing idea across the frontier. He deals confidently with the "Psychology of the mob," and "the aggregate mind," and the hypnotic influence of the crowd. There is such an air of authority about it all, that we forget that he is dealing with figures of speech. On the other hand, the Sociologist attempts to solve the most delicate problems of the individual soul by the statistical method.

EQUALITY

"All men are created equal"

Thomas Jefferson

Every man is born equal. Equal to whom, or what? Equal to his self, to be sure. In Putnam's Monthly of October 1853, a physician wrote, "The private judgment of the individual is the only safe criterion, and he should be answerable only to this own sense of right and wrong. This is the soul of our code of ethics. All that our associations and authoritative conventions demand, is, that each should concede to others this liberty of opinion. Such is the republic of medicine—truest of all republics, holding perfect individual freedom consistent with the safety of all."

Where can I find the residence of *my* fellow man if not within my self? To locate the abode of my governmental authority elsewhere than within me, is an acknowledgement of my inability to abide my governmental meanings with composure, an instance of my inability to feel equal to my self.

There can be no consciousness other than self consciousness. My full consciousness is my awareness for my existence which identifies me inseparably with my self. My sense of my personal identity in all of my living is my equalizer. My sense of equality (to my own living) is my sense of sanity. Without the functioning of my full self consciousness, I must live myself as irreconcilable diversities, as a body of contradictions, as a "scatterbrain" complaining that I am the butt of "circumstances."

The central interest of every human life with regard to each of its experiences is, How can I regulate it and not have it regulate me? How can I extend my conscious self sovereignty to comprehend it, and not have it seem to rule my life? How can I achieve self control and not surrender to a tail-wagging-the-dog life orientation? How can I feel up to living my own life? The idea behind this central interest of every human being is: I am the creator of all of my creations, any one of which threatens to become a frankenstein to the extent that I cannot see my very own identity in it, and thus see myself "grow equal" to it. Equally, every American citizen creates his own democratic government.

Despite the oft-made declaration that it cannot be clearly explained, or scientifically justified, there is nothing mysterious in the expression "the equality of men," provided that such an idea of plurality is not used to repress the only human truth: the individuality of man. Nothing is, or can be, sanely explicable on the basis of "betweeness." Every such term implying plurality calls man's inviolable organic wholeness in question, thus reducing his true greatness to illusional littleness. Omar Bradley phrased the resulting picture, "Ours is a world of nuclear giants and ethical infants."

Each man is his own all, and therefore must be equal to his self. Equality means identity, sameness. The complete, full grown American citizen is equal to realizing his "then" and "there" creations as self observations. He sees how he can use "there" and "then" to repress *here* and *now*. He does not suffer from the illusion that the seat of his government is in one place and that he is in another place. He does not measure himself merely as an infinitesimal speck in a vast universe. He is neither a space-server nor a time-server, and thereby escapes all of the tangled webs which such self deceptions as "space," "past," and "future" must weave.

My basic assumption in American government of the principle of equality, perhaps more than any other, offers me clear view of the humaneness of American citizenship. In all sanity, "equality" cannot mean that one person is in any sense equal or unequal to another person. In the one sense that the whole appears greater than any one of its elements, every American citizen must acknowledge that his mind subsumes all of his meaning for his fellow citizen. It is rare for a human being to recognize that he is equal to his self, but his awareness or lack of awareness for this truth cannot impugn its actuality.

Every citizen capable of comprehending *his* fellow citizen as an existent within him, cannot but uphold his fellow citizen's claim to "equal protection" under the law. Every citizen who lives *his* fellow citizen as if he is not an existent within him,

needs motivation other than that consciously provided by his
sense of personal identity for upholding his fellow citizen's right
to "equal protection" under the law. Thus arises his need for
"force of law and order" that he cannot recognize as his own.

Usage has made the term "citizen" nearly synonymous with
the term "voter." Usage describes the citizen as a member of the
body politic. It is well to see clearly the greatly limited helpfulness in such belittling designation of American citizenship.
Actually the term citizen can mean only: One who duly
acknowledges as his very own living of it, the government indicated by his citizenship. In order for a citizen to grow the
government of his choice as his very own conscious living of it,
he must grow himself in such a way as to create this insightful
living. To wit, he must meet the so-called requirement of citizenship: of arousing his mind enough to perceive that he is equal to
its meanings.

Every citizen incapable of being aware that he must live his
fellow citizen as his self, requires himself to live some kind of
pacific power other than that which he can call his own will
power. Usual designation of this imagined kind of pacific power
is: police force. "In modern America, an effective police force is
vastly more important than it was in former times. As our civilization has changed from rural to urban, we have turned over
more and more of its burdens to the police—far more than most
people recognize."*

Jeremy Bentham's ideal was, "Every man his own lawyer."
He carefully pointed out the reliable peace officers of human
being: "Nature has placed mankind under the governance of
two sovereign masters, pain and pleasure. It is for them alone to
point out what we ought to do, as well as to determine what we
shall do." One cannot but wonder, would Kant, Rousseau, and
many another one, have denied the dependability of self interest
as a reputable moral motive, had each one lived a democratic

*_The Police on the Urban Frontier_, by George Edwards, Judge, U. S. Court of
Appeals, for the Sixth Circuit, Institute of Human Relations Press, 165 E.
56th Street, New York, 10022, 1968. An urgently needed clarification.

government? Yet Locke and Hobbes, and innumerable others, each developed much of this insight without benefit of democratic citizenship. And Rousseau himself began his Social Contract: "By what inconceivable art has a means been found of making men free by making them subject?"

THE MAJORITY RULE

"Any man more right than his neighbor, constitutes a majority of one."

Henry David Thoreau

Knowing that what matters is only concrete individuality, Aristotle said man may be described as a political animal, that is, as one who is conscious of his need to live his fellowman peacefully. In the life process of his self growth he cannot help but create (within himself) the unified identity known as his fellowman. If he can see his life as all his own, he cannot help but sense that his functioning of self consciousness can proceed freely; he will very soon come to recognize the necessity for self governing contrivances, for ideal political condition in his life. As Charles S. Myers asserted,* "no reputable psychologist can be found today who believes that mental processes as we know them occur outside the living organism."

A democratic citizen must create all of his mental devices for making democracy work. He must alert himself not to lose his mind (forget himself) in his politics. Thus, he must see that his every committee can be only a committee of one, of himself. Each sufficiently self conscious person growing himself as a committee member, sees that he lives all that occurs in his committee experience. He does not call majority rule a sway of some "external" force. His sensing his own identity in each one of his committee members, gives his majority vote a humanistic meaning which it could not possibly have otherwise. *"Social obligation" is self opportunity.* Now is the only lifetime.

Diplomat Raymond Blaine Fosdick noted, "It is always the minorities that hold the key of progress; it is always through those who are unafraid to be different that advance comes to human society." The citizen who sees the humaneness of majority rule may vote with his minority, but this comprehensive view

In the Realm of Mind, 1937.

of his human life clearly indicates to him that his majority has a greater right of human life on its side, and that this specific right makes all of the might in his majority. Furthermore, his awareness of the human life involved (his own), creates the necessity for his pacific solution of the overpowering weight of his human opposition, as of his every governmental problem. Patriotic feeling for responsible self control awakens with trust of mind.

The competency of majority rule is not, as Edmund Burke implied it to be, a "problem of arithmetic." Instead, the majority view is only important as *one* considerable fact in the mind of the viewer. I am apt to recognize in it a beneficial respect for some of my living I have slighted. All of my obligation to my fellowman lives in my obligation to my self, and it functions most effectively with that realization. Amplification of my conscious self identity solves my every "social" problem.

Political equality for *my* fellowman is most natural. Universal suffrage for *my* self economy is most desirable. This fact is not less true because "the great majority of human beings" may be lacking in political insight. Recognized benefit of universal suffrage is needed to awaken everyone's consciousness about the need for self education to self realization. Only daring conscious self experience can rescue my dormant devotion to my democratic ideal.

It is not only the privilege but the duty of every American to be concerned about the efficiency of his government. No part of his democratic system can be wholesomely free from his personal scrutiny. William Henry Harrison affirmed, "A decent and manly examination of the acts of Government should be not only tolerated, but encouraged."

Only a human individual has a human mind. A "majority of the people" has no mind at all. It seems evident enough that "majority opinion" regarding any human issue, such as "sexuality," "criminality," or "the law" is sufficiently mindless, irresponsible, to warrant most careful and continuing heed. For example, the whole force of "punishment" for infraction of "the law" always operates to excite further infraction, and never to deter it. The scientist of his mind discovers that punishment always begets punishment, never compliance. Nevertheless "punishment" continues to be the inexorable demand of "the majority of the people." The attainment of individual sex control through loving education is the sure solution for any and every sexual "problem." Nevertheless. a policy of ignoration continues to be the wish of "the majority of the people." Every insightful educator observes that the purpose of his mind is to enable him to cultivate every possible kind of human experience with understanding for its necessity (desirability, helpfulness). The mind which has strengthened itself to heed *whatever is* as precious life lesson, does not "go to pieces," "fly off the handle," "faint," or otherwise indicate its unpreparedness for difficult living. Nevertheless, more or less "soft" easy unchallenging ever-pleasing "customary" experience, continues to constitute "the ideal way of life" for "the majority of the people."

That every kind of so-called "social problem" is traceable directly to shortsighted conception of the meaning of "the majority of the people," is the demonstrably valid but overlooked fact. A view of "the majority of the people" that depicts it to be greater than a human individual is absolutely incompatible with any adequate definition of "normality" or "morality" or "law." Indeed, "the majority of the people" cannot be (do) anything, except one meaning in the life of any individual who gives it his momentary valuable consideration. This all-important truth can be created only by and in the mind of a daringly insightful human individual.

Since my American government is my very own personal arrangement of my mind for realizing the inviolable truth of my self sovereignty, enabling my human individuality to revere its self; since my American government exists all and only in its citizen; since the fully workable policy for my respecting my individuality coincides with my fully respecting my every one; and since my "rule of the majority" enables my respecting my own individuality to the fullest possible extent; therefore, it is most essential for my true patriotism that I understand my "majority rule" as *my* own best self governmental provision, and *not* as some kind of exception to my one and only governmental possibility, my self sovereignty.

"Coercion" (such as any kind of seeming "external necessity" or "internal compulsion") cannot exist at all except as the individual mind conceives (creates) it for its self. Every kind of infraction of law is understandable only as a cry for self help which lawbreaker and lawmaker may not recognize as such. Like the child who needs to live *his* parent as if an "external" (rather than actually as his own internal) control, the so-called criminal needs to use his governmental peace officer as if an "external involuntary" source of self help. *His* peace officer seems "outside" to him, quite as he can imagine all of his difficult unhappy living as seeming "outside." He cannot yet tolerate the fact that he *is* his dislikes just as he is his likes. "Growing up" is the result of discovering that accepted "growing pain" is worth while for it is the only sufferance that can extend conscious self love in one's very own self world. All of consciousness is sensibility for one's self only.

Really there is only one possible "majority," namely, the given individual. He it is who subsumes all of the illusional plurality seemingly implied in the pluralistic term. *My* sovereign State or United Nations derives all of its "sovereignty" from my self sovereignty. Every individual may be considered as a kind of home for his nurture of his world experience. As insightful United States Commissioner of Education William T. Harris upheld the precious reality of solipsism,

> Give scepticism the rein, make it as thorough as possible, and the result is a subjective idealism, which affirms that the mind cannot know anything but its own forms or ideas.

Any so-called "Democratic process" exists all and only in the given individual mind creating it. "The People" has no mind at all, if the mind which conceives the meaning of the term is excluded. No process whatsoever can occur in "the people." No process whatsoever can occur in any so-called "plurality." "Plurality," itself, is a term for a phantastic conception which presumably negates "individuality." My every "plural" is nothing but my *single* conception of my notion "more-than-one." My term "part" also implies "plurality" but it also is a term for a phantastic conception which negates individuality even as it appears to posit it. Every so-called "part" is *wholly* its self.

It is only sanity to study and practice the fact that every collective noun and every plural term has absolutely no existence whatsoever but its existence in the *individual* human being's vocabulary. The resulting insightful self understanding from such health education, is the one and only source for recognizable humaneness! As long as I, all-being individual that I am, hypnotize myself with my seemingly self foreign terms (such as "the people," "the government," "the many," "society," "the environment," "the family," "the church," or "externality" of any kind or degree whatsoever), I shall continue to experience my helpful distressing unhappiness warning me of my *effort to negate* some of my undeniable self sovereignty. However, again, "the majority of the people" (be "they" educators, statesmen, clergymen, philanthropists, or of any other such seemingly "plural" constitution) cannot be of any kind or degree of help in heeding this all-important consideration, for "they" do not and cannot even exist, except as several terms for phantastic denial of the very truth of individuality itself.

I can send my governor or my president a copy of my carefully worked-up view of the inviolability of individuality (such as this one) fully realizing that he may judge it his due responsibility to consider it, not as his own work-up nor as a work-up of anyone but just one of his "many millions of fellow citizens." Meanwhile I may literally live in hope for the coming of the insight that the direst need exists for continuous intensive mind awakening of every government official, specifically in the direction of his cultivating his appreciation that his every "constituent" (or committee member, "legislative, judiciary, or executive representative," and so on) is absolutely nothing but what his very own dear life makes of such *self sovereignty* device. My every word can only reveal or conceal me.

Each insightful philologist cannot but discover the dangerous extent to which he has had to help his self by resort to his semantic psychosis, "depersonalization." He can gradually awaken sufficiently to recognize his chief symptom under his own diagnosis of self *tapinosis*. Yet, even my sophisticated educator may not be awake to the profoundly personal meaningfulness of self belittlement named in this all too rarely appreciated and hardly ever listed term.

SEPARATION OF POWERS

"What do you suppose will satisfy the soul, except to walk free and
own no superior?"

Walt Whitman

All that can be meant by "separation" is distinctification.
American political sagacity distinctifies autonomy as much as
possible. Thus, church and state are separate; medicine is practiced privately; home and school are respected as "separate"
entites; local "grass roots" educational jurisdiction is upheld;
each executive, judiciary, or legislative power is autonomous;
and so on.

Only my self consciousness can enable me to see clearly that I
have, or have not, reached a stage of my political development
where I have sufficient civic wisdom to sense my responsiblity as
a voter, "separate" in the sense of belonging to myself. The level
of my politics is essentially the level of my realization that my
public interest is entirely a private interest of mine, for instance,
that my "spoils-based" political organization is nothing but my
personal living of it. It is my mental power that creates in my
one mind every so-called "separate" existential realm.

Specializing in my conscious individualism (if I do), I benefit
from this intensely personal "localism" in innumerable governmental ways, every one of which reveals the full truth of autonomy. To illustrate, if I am content to live only a part of my
government such as my "Supreme Court" as having the power
to control the constitutional guarantees of the liberty of all of
me, I clearly suffer an impairment of mental vision about what
autonomy means. The necessity for individualization of each
and every power, and hence the advantage in observing such
"separation," is the product of extensive (rather than limited)
self consciousness.

In all of my living I find indispensable to my strengthening my
wish to live, this insight: so-called evil is good, not understood. I
must renounce my self blinding tendency to confuse *whatever* I

67

live with dislike, as evidence of the existence of evil. Abraham Kaplan states it thus, "What the absolute moralist calls 'dirty politics' is its natural condition. The politician is the scapegoat for what an absolute morality regards as the sin of compromise. But when a necessity of nature becomes sinful, it is the morality that is unnatural."

Free self interest discovers that education for American citizenship involves a kind appreciation and tender treatment of potentially dangerous unconscious personifications such as "political pressure," "the Press slanting the news," "drugged individualism," "racketeering," "enemy of the people," "kickbacks," "stockwatering," "jury packing," "judicial spoils," "all the traffic will bear," "party politics," "the state," "big business," "the corporation," "the school board," "supreme court," and so on and on. Observing such views as nothing but my own life's expressions is all that can save me from a self unconscious life of verbalism (so-called, "communication"). I must look in vain for an honest man until I learn to look in the only place where I can really *see,* in my self.

A prized possession of every American citizen is his governmental system of "checks and balances," made possible by the "separation of powers." The most practical application of this democratic instrument is its usefulness in seeing to it that the "professional" does not ignore his identity with his fellow citizen who is a layman. Thus, every American maintains his sense of authority with regard to his professional educator, statesman, soldier, and so on; and each "professional" maintains his sense of identity with his fellow citizen the layman.

Pointing out to the members of Congress, the need for each Cabinet member to identify his self responsibly with the work of the member of each House, President William Howard Taft observed of the "separation" of executive, legislative and judicial powers, "It was never intended that they should be separated in the sense of not being in constant effective touch and relationship to each other."

Obviously the professional scientist by the simple means of making a tabu of the "personal" in science, circumvented this system of checks and balances. Then fortified with his own broken principle that dislike must not bias his acceptance of truth, he proceeded to dissociate his scientific self from his identity with his fellow layman. My "scientific" lethal weapons now threaten the preservation of my human existence.

Abraham Lincoln

MY UNITED SELF

"In the beginning the world was nothing but the Atman, in the form
of a man. It looked around and saw nothing different to itself. Then it
cried out once, 'It is I.' That is how the word 'I' came to be."

Upanishad-Brihadaranyaka

By "self" I refer to my whole creaturehood, my entire individuality, experiencing its viability. By "mind" I refer to any
and all *meaning* of my living. Insightful Destutt de Tracy
(1754–1836), greatly esteemed both by Thomas Jefferson and
John Adams for his mental acuity, coined the term "Ideology"
to refer to his analysis of individual sensibility:

> "The *self* of each of us is for him his proper sensibility, whatsoever be
> the nature of this sensibility; or what he calls mind, if he has a
> decided opinion of the nature of the principle of this same sensiblity.
> It is so true that it is this that we all understand by *self*, that we all
> regard apparent death as the end of our being . . . according as we
> think it extinguishes all sentiment. It is then the sole fact of sensibil-
> ity which gives us the idea of personality, that is which makes us
> perceive that we are a *being*, and which constitutes for us ourself, our
> being."*

Even as I write these words on self authority and responsiblity, July 27, 1967, my beautiful American day is fiercely aloud
with violent noises of piercing sirens, harsh voices and reports of
guns,—all signifying *my* black or white fellow citizen's devotion
to his blinding delusion of "race" at the cost of disregard for his
one and only insightful truth, his *individuality*. On New Year's
Day, 1967, *The New York Times* reporter insightfully stated:
"Race is a slippery, misleading often dangerous word, scientists
said at a symposium here (at a meeting of the American Association for the Advancement of Science). Some speakers urged

*"*Elements of Ideology,*" 1817, Translated from French by Thomas Jefferson
who commented, "The merit of this work will, I hope, place it in the hands of
every reader in our country."

that the word be abandoned altogether in studies involving human populations." As already asserted "race" is merely a name for a meaning existing *only* in the mind inventing that word. Furthermore, whatever meaning it names, concerns *only* the mind in which it occurs. *My awareness for this significance of my every word, as being merely but mightily a name for a meaning created by and in my own mind, is my most helpful semantic possession.*

I am observing my mind and recording its meaning in my effort to steady and strengthen it right now, just when I need to depend upon its conscious power, in order to be as helpful as I can be for the welfare of my presently disturbed neighborhood. I am a *conscious* self educator. Every scientist of my world is of necessity a self educator and may help himself greatly by realizing that he *is* all he observes.

I have found immense value in educating my self appreciation to be able to recognize my self *particularly* in every person I observe. I consider my *all* to be in my mind and integral to it; my mind must be all and only in itself. Whether I use the classical gross or modern atomic concepts of time, space, motion or substance, each concept is a construct in my personal speculation. If I do allow my "rhetorical form" to substitute itself for my individuality awareness, then I must suffer the consequence of such a dangerous distortion,—mind blindness instead of mind sight. Professor C. S. Broad, author of *The Mind and Its Place in Nature,* writes:

> Whenever we are told that "Science proves so-and-so to be impossible" we must remember that this is merely a rhetorical form of "Professor X and most of his colleagues assert so-and-so to be impossible." Those of us who have the privilege of meeting Professor X and his colleagues daily, and know from experience what kinds of assertions they are capable of making when they leave their own subject, will, I am afraid, remain completely unmoved.

I take pride in my acknowledgeable American self sovereignty that entitles and enables me to appreciate my comprehensive view of my wholeness oneness and allness. Professor George Herbert Palmer recorded, "A scholar is hardly grown up until he makes another language and another national outlook his own." For instance, my American scholar may and can make his Russian language and national outlook his own. Does my Russian fellowman's educational or psychological orientation encourage this mental liberty? *A restricted mind cannot live itself kindly in the area excluded by its restrictions.*

True, conscious self sovereignty is evidently the most difficultly attained and maintained civil government of all that a citizen may try. True, the peaceful balance of self authority and self responsibility is most difficultly worked up. True, the American citizen must teach himself painful lessons that his civic land of liberty, like his religious Kingdom of God, can exist only within him. True, manworthy conscious self sovereignty is the fruitage only of self discipline specifically in extending self identity, that tries the patience of the saint. True, every objection featuring the enormous difficulty always before every person who would strive to call his soul his own and his all his soul. *But all I have to do to keep at my man's work of learning to see only myself in all of my wonderful world, is to consider my awful alternative!*

Twenty-five years ago, after living through a similar painful lesson on rioting in my home town, being a conscious self educator, I wrote promptly down my sober experienced understanding of all of the so-called "mob rioting" as being nothing but the consequence of each individual rioter's limited conscious self appreciation (his limited *conscious* self identity).* In other words, I called my attention to the inability of my white rioter to see that he *is* his only black, or of my black rioter to see that he *is* his only white.

At great length I then described how hostility for my "others" is nothing but my own injured self love; how my intolerance for intolerance is no improvement upon intolerance for so-called "color"; how every "white" *is* a white black just as every "black" is a black white; how either love or hate or any other feeling, is all about itself and cannot modify *any* other "subject" or "object" or so-called "externality"; how my *every* emotion is my strictly personal physiological experience having *no possible*

*"*A Psychotherapeutic Approach to the Problem of Hostility"*, "Social Forces," Dec., 1950.

meaning whatsoever for anyone but me; how my life of nonviolent peace must be one of sanity founded upon my study and practice of my very own *self identity* in all of my experience of any kind or degree whatsoever; how my realistic solution of every so-called "race problem" is not accessible to my mind's "reasoning" but only to my mind's self awareness (known also as "self consciousness" or "self insight"); how my use of "reasoning" can favor my illusion of being able to get at or be gotten at by my fellowman of whatever color; how only the functioning of my self awareness can awaken me to the indispensable truth of the inviolability of my individuality; and so on. I am the only "black" or "white" I can ever see or know anything about. Modifying Jefferson's cry for unity, We are all black, we are all white!

For years as University Professor I have offered a course of study entitled, The Psychology of Successful Living, during which I describe my lifelong efforts to help my self realize the truly amazing wonderfulness of my human nature. I picture my most marvelous achievements to be 1) my being alive and 2) my being aware that I am alive. There is no condition of my life worthier of the title of "success" than my realization that *success* is all that is possible in human nature, that so-called "failure" is always merely unrecognized success. I state my most consequential life understanding is my realization that my growing a strong mind is my most difficult accomplishment. It can be achieved only in one way, I add, simply by my cultivating perseveringly and painstakingly my insight that my life is all and only about me. My rioting going on right now, to the extent that it is being lived by me, is being created by me. I am painfully responsible for being it.

All of my life experience *is* my life's being, and I *can* induce myself to discipline my mind with my self consciousness. Such mental discipline, most difficult but also most rewarding, constitutes my civic and ethical principle. I identify my life orientation in saying with my Marcus Aurelius, "O Universe! what thou wishest I wish." To work up my clearsighted conviction and to dare to be of my evident opinion of *how life is appropriately lived;* to stand up for it bravely for *my* own world,—this is the core meaning of my United States citizenship as of my basic ethical power, of my moral *ought*. I am ethical according to my developed views of self help. This choice insight reveals the unique worthwhileness in my activating my ethical principle. The divine egotism I call my "morality" creates a tendency of my mind favorable to mental activity furthering my welfare, generating my motive to do right by my self world, be it black or white, male or female, or whatever.

Looking up from my writing, distracted by the clanging of my fire engines and patrol wagons speeding towards billowing smoke and bellowing citizen, I can observe my fine black neighbor, a self respecting man, calmly, quietly, courteously going about his business as usual, but also awake to deep concern for the welfare of *all* of his home town. Then for a while again I overwhelm my mind by returning to its exciting views, until *I* can once more come to my senses by means of arousing my self consciousness. Understandably I feel compelling urge to extend my helpfulness into *my* world, and only my strictest mental discipline in self insight enables me to heed the truth that my one and only way to increase my helpfulness of any kind, is by growing greater appreciation for the wonderful worth of my own life.

For many years now the literature I have made with love has been of a most unique nature in that it features the soul of human reality, namely, *conscious* individual human being its self. To the best of my ability I have elaborated this one and only specifically humanizing viewpoint in all of my writing, painfully aware that it is the desperately needed desideratum in nearly all educational efforts of my fellowman. Today as much as three hundred and fifty years ago, the sense in the quatrain of Sir John Davies can be created only by the rare self conscious mind,

> We that acquaint ourselves with every Zone
> And pass both Tropics and behold the Poles,
> When we come home are to ourselves unknown,
> And unacquainted still with our own Souls.

A first consideration in understanding my rioting, a view too rarely and fleetingly perceived by me, is to incline myself, however painfully, to *full appreciation for its beneficence*. I cannot secure this kind of self "education" from my formal schooling. Professor James Harvey Robinson observed in 1922,

> It is quite true that what we need is education, but something so different from what now passes as such that it needs a new name.

That name must indicate that the pupil is weakening his mind by any learning that he cannot or does not recognize as being his own mental development, as his growing and forming his own mind's powers; and that the pupil is strengthening his mind by any learning that he can or does recognize as being his self experience shaping his mind with his self consciousness. The former "impersonalism" study seems easy; the latter "personal" study is hard for it requires the continuous enlarging of the pupil's conscious self identity.

Once "calm and collected," I again realize that the only news I have ever been able to recognize as "having come from heaven," has come to me through my appreciation for my self consciousness. Acknowledging my own resistance to struggling and striving to see only my own self identity in my "impoverished" rioter, I cannot now fail to understand my overburdened rioter's resistance to seeing only his own self identity in his seemingly "well off" fellowman.

In my world, neither my poor nor rich man seems aware that his sole and whole possession is self possession; that only increase of self consciousness can bring the "mental backing" behind life satisfaction; that his world of self is his only possible source of providence; that he lives in bondage to his belief in help other than self help, holdings other than self productions, consciousness other than self consciousness; that his amount of self identity is not a fixed quantity allowing no expansion; that his power of reasoning is not as safe a life-guide as is his self consciousness; that when he becomes conscious for more of his mind he becomes conscious for more of his abundance; that the open secret of consciously successful living is to discover there is no kind of meaning whatsoever except *that* one's self creates by and about one's self; that one sleeps his life away except to the extent that he is awake to his selfhood; that extending awareness for personal identity is increasing conscious will power, furthering organic functioning to enjoy, freeing wisdom to understand how to continue working one's mind in keeping with one's love of life.

It is only natural for me to believe in the goodness of whatever *obviously* seems to help me. I cannot vitalize my self by a belief in my shortsightedness, particularly since it *seems* to me that my very own facts of my life do not and cannot sufficiently account for, and completely justify, my misery and desperation. I try to identify my good in the good of my whole world, but insightful, beautiful revelations such as Edwin Markham's exasperate me as long as my attention must be devoted to my suffering," Only the soul that knows the mighty grief can know the mighty rapture. Sorrows come to stretch out spaces in the heart for joy."

The supreme, amazing power of truth, awareness for the truth as being *my* truth, must remain undiscovered by me, as long as I keep myself from knowing what it alone can do for me in revealing my absolute wholeness allness and oneness for their due honor and glory. Until I difficultly work up this kind and degree of self realization, I must satisfy myself with a limited concept of my self identity that is incompatible with my whole truth of my nature and irreconcilable with my full love for my wonderful life. Thus I force myself to go on riotously spending my life's energy, ignoring the truth that any "loss" in my world is my "loss", disregarding the truth that any gain in my world is my gain. Although my consciously "putting on the new man" in no respect means "getting rid of the old man," it is regularly experienced as if my life depends upon my self identity's maintaining its *status quo*.

Enterprise for this death-defying work of continuously giving birth to my true self identity is itself an issue of my convincing myself of its benefit to me. Once I can see clearly that "apparent unselfishness" is identical with *real* self interest, then I not only can, but also I feel I must, devote myself to it as worthy labor of self love. Once I can see that the truth of my subjectivity provides all of the illusion of my "objectivity," I learn how to make the most of *conscious* living, how to secure in consciously increasing measure the attainment of my life's true purpose of fulfilling its very own marvelously perfect universe of self. Somewhat as self confiding Ralph Waldo Emerson recorded, When the half gods go the great God arrives.

As is every other ethic, so mine is my application to my conduct of my conception of my world. Thus, if I conceive my rioting fellowman right now as doing all that he can do in view of his present facilities, then instead of blaming him, I can apply such guilt to my feeling responsible for helping my self to live my disturbing experience with saner appreciation for the reality of forceful fact accounting for it fully. Before I grew mental strength to consider all of *my* world as made up entirely of my own living, I had to take care of it with conscious responsibility only to whatever extent I *could* recognize it as my owndom. Thus, as black I was not able to see *only* my self in my living of my white fellowman; or as white I was unable to see *only* my self in my living of my black fellowman. As male, I was unable to see *only* my self in my experiencing my female living; and as female I was unable to see *only* my self in my living of my male fellowman. And so on. I could not appreciate as being only my own individual existence, whatever unpleasant living of mine I had not difficultly awakened myself to recognize as entirely my very own.

My first published research on the meaning of "race" rioting received highest commendation from the editor who accepted it for publication, as well as from the awake reader already prepared to see it as his own self orientation. However it was and remains, like this publication, uniquely unsuitable for use by the so-called "mass" approach of my organization man, such as my formal educator for instance. My philosophy as an "organization man" is dead set against the realistic ethical ideal of my self as a conscious individual man. However my self loving insight reveres each view as precious human living.

As I now create the mounting excitements of shout, shot and siren, I find it necessary to renounce every natural temptation to turn and run towards all of the turmoil. Conducting my life as usual, as a peacemaking person, seems clearly the difficult choice. I calm my self with my awareness that although I am responsible for all of my rioting of my fellowman, I am also responsible for all of the rest of the world that I live. I resume my earnest effort to understand 1) what kind of use of my mind favors my rioting and 2) what kind of use of my mind favors my self responsibly creating my personal identity. Nothing can quell my rioter's violence effectively except his awakening further to the extent of his self identity.

However, over the years my so-called "materialistic" philosopher has regularly resisted the very concept of his own personal identity. Lichtenberg, "the philosopher of impersonality," later corrected his own mental position "I think" into "It thinks," considering a personal ego to be merely a grammatical creation. Epistemologist Ernst Mach observed his holistic organicity to the extent of identifying the content of his perceptions as *the* realities of his mind. Even David Hume described his mind as a bundle of several perceptions in constant ebb and flow.

Whenever any strong mind overwhelms itself with excitation, it regresses from its consciously idealistic subjective individual position to its unconscious materialistic objective plural or partial position. Whenever I cannot assume responsibility for my own mental creations, I fall back upon my illusion of dependence upon my "others" that I cannot recognize as elements of my own self identity.

Identifying my ethic with my *conscious* self knowledge, means that any and all of my learning or self experience (including every kind or degree of my scientific discovery) has built into it the ethical injunction of my self concern. Thus all of my riotous living *is* I but must be fully acknowledged as I, before it is willingly (consciously) appreciated with my self love. Meanwhile, all of my self repudiation is performed in the interest of maintaining whatever conscious self love I *can* tolerate. From my consciousness-alienated mental power, my "mob-mindedness" derives all of its force. To the degree that I consider myself a member of society, rather than consider my "society" a member of my societal self, my appreciation for my self sovereignty is obscured.

No mental attitude is more demoralizing than that of feeling unable to help my self, a most distressing life view that is excited and aggravated by my cherished illusion that one person can help (or be helped by) another. My illusion of either helping or hurting others is indulged at the exorbitant expense of 1) realizing my precious lifelong ability to help myself and 2) overlooking the priceless individuality-respecting truth that only my fellowman *can* help himself. For instance, to be reality oriented, any "anti-poverty" program of mine must be conducted with this insight *ever* operative: *There is no possible help ever but self help.* Charity begins and stays at home in the individual living it.

My first pamphlet on individual man's riotous living pointed out how "punitive measures" merely aggravate the dangerous "law-breaking" symptoms of the agonized so-called "criminal" individual; and how firm and sufficiently powerful (but pacific) force must be available so that the raving, rioting individual can use it to help himself gradually to his conscious self control. Again, a self rioting citizen needs to live his powerful but nonviolent *self controlled* peace officer for his own guiding and guarding of his conduct, quite as a child needs *his* loving but forceful parent for this same source of his self development towards his *conscious* self sovereignty. Furthermore my insightless individual's mob-mindedness can subdue itself 1) by experiencing what it conceives to be a "more powerful mob," and 2) by each mobber's experiencing the self consciousness that dispels his "mob" illusion. My ethical moment enabling me to renounce my wish to live riotously, is all and only the expression of my obligation to let my self consciousness function freely.

My propounding my most simple ethical theory cannot result in my every individual's abandoning his own ingenious speculation about the meaning of his selfhood, nor would such "abandoning" be desirable. The most my fellow self educator can do with regard to his author's conscious self view would be to *add* it to his already consciously appropriated self experience. An ethical self world is an invention of one's imaginative power of self observation, not an hypothesis. It is based upon conscious self data and applied to conscious self data. Conscious self data, the only evident realities of human living, ethically idealize: Whatever is, ought to be. Only self consciousness *can* realize the ideal. Searching the skies, or "seeing America first," or "going abroad," is no exception to looking into myself. In myself I live and move, and have all of my being.

If I have not worked my mind into the position to see clearly the self deluding power in whatever I call "foreign" or "plural," I must continue to depend upon such phantoms of mind. My spirit of ethics is found in the motto of my Country: *E Pluribus Unum*. However, "One is all, all is one." is wisdom generated only by self insight. For my "objectivity" minded brother, it must seem exactly as impractical and unrealistic as does that glorious insight, Love thy neighbor as thyself, or, Love thy enemy. Meanwhile the one who has succeeded in teaching himself the rare realization that his altruism *is* his grown-up egotism, and that his egotism is all that there is (or can be) to depend upon for his decision making, *that* one has learned to renounce such soft solutions for human want as "sharing his wisdom" or "imparting his knowledge" or "teaching the 'multitudes' ". Frantic resorts of his fellowman to imaginary self help other than conscious self development are regularly *expected* by him. He understands desperate efforts of his neighbor to attain by easy "social legislation" or riotous force, what *can* be attained only by the kind but fearsome force of acknowledgeable self awakening. He comprehends how all such enticing "community," "group" or "mob" alternatives must seem preferable to the hard work of discovering that the *difficult* conscious living of human individuality is the only possible solution for each and every human demand for human "freedom," "equality," "justice," "opportunity," "power," or whatever.

Just as the consciously self oriented one is unsurprised by his fellowman's shortsighted resort to violence, neither is he upset by his fellowman "in power" and "on the side of the law" who must feel overwhelmed instead of admittedly self awakened by his law-breaking fellowman, who cannot understand that riotous behavior must result only from the specific self condition of suffering human *individuality* necessitating it.

In all of this seeking of self helpfulness through conscious self helpfulness, there is one point to be understood well. Man is

potentially a self conscious man and it is his birthright to strive
and strive to guide himself by his consciousness for the wonderfulness of his creaturehood. He cannot safely or sanely disregard
this inborn responsibility, however difficult his effort to live up
to it may be. Fortunate is his self experience if it pushes this self
knowledge to the front of his life interest, so that it can be given
the attention its life importance demands and deserves. If the
salt of the earth has lost its savor wherewith shall it be salted?
Only the human individual *can* savor human life, his own.
Human individuality must have its way. Finding out just what
that way is, in order to appreciate and regulate it, is the best
possible work for the idealist devoted to his "cause of humanity." This hard-earned self insight leads to the following one.

The very idea most needed for restoring mental balance following great pain (unhappiness of any kind) reveals: *living a
human life is the most difficult of all conceivable difficulties.*
This sanity-restoring life understanding too rarely has a chance
even to be considered. However this necessary consequence of
the immense power of human individuality (namely, that power
is as power does) is ever operative whether consciously or unconsciously. For my individual human welfare, my only kind of
human welfare possible, I constantly need this life understanding to be *consciously* operative. It is uniquely in my awakening
to my inherent greatness and goodness that I need to school my
united self.

I explain to myself how it happens that I am thus far a moral
being able to renounce rioting, as follows: All that can be know-
able about "knowledge" is that it is an observation of self meaning in a human being. Each knowing one *is* the only subject of
his knowledge. Just to the extent that I am aware that all of my
knowledge is entirely and only about myself, can I be aware of
my intact wholeness, of the innocence of my ethical self. However, insofar as I ignore my knowledge as being my self meaning, I must be vulnerable to an obsessive mental attitude that I
ought to live myself consciously (responsibly rather than guilt-
ily). My "voice of conscience" is my calling upon myself to realize that my life *is* my own, and that my all *is* my living of my
self.

I can imagine that man might be the only earthly creature who is capable of feeling unethical, since he alone clearly appears to be able to delude himself that his living, or being, is not entirely and only his own. Self consciousness is the quality of human individuality that makes man an ethical being. Self unconsciousness is the source of all "unethical" living. In difficultly becoming aware that I am victim just as I am victor, or "loser" just as I am winner, or "sinner" just as I am saint, and so on, I learn 1) how to restore myself to ethical living (to my early innocence characterizing my not denying my own living in my self experience) and 2) how to transform my unconscious involuntary activity into my conscious will-power. This ethic of full-measured self appreciation (consciousness) is the specific one that conforms to "the good will" of Kant's ethics, in that it is the one and only maxim of conduct that may become universal law.

My description of the desperate helpfulness in the frantic mind's resort to self rioting, attempts to study "race" rioting (or any "mob" action) where it is actually occurring, namely, all and only in the mind of the so-called "racist" (or "mobber") who is currently incapable of acknowledging that his world is all and only his individual world. There can be no such possibility as one's ever having anything to do with a so-called "race" or "mob". This insight, the one most needed for individual human welfare, must seem a "far-fetched impractical notion" to my fellowman who has had to help himself extensively by limiting the range of his self consciousness. Here is what Michigan's most insightful sociologist, Professor Charles Horton Cooley, has to say on that head:*

> I conclude that the imaginations which people have of one another
> are the solid facts of society, and that to observe and interpret these
> must be the chief aim of sociology. I do not mean merely that society
> must be studied by the imagination—that is true of all investigations
> in their higher reaches—but that the object of study is primarily an
> imaginative idea or group of ideas in the mind, that we have to imag-

*Human Nature and the Social Order, Charles Scribner's Sons, New York 1922, (pp. 121–122)

83

ine imaginations. . . . It is important to face the question of persons who have no corporeal reality, as for instance the dead, characters of fiction or the drama, ideas of the gods and the like. Are these real people, members of society? I should say that insofar as we imagine them they are.

Professor Cooley goes on to point out that it "is healthy for every one to understand that he is, and will remain, a self-seeker, and that if he gets out of one self he is sure to form another which may stand in equal need of control." This kind of conception of altruism as being enlarged egoism, is of the greatest possible importance for my renouncing my resort to violence when I feel hurt. I can be violent only with my own life, regardless of all appearances to the contrary. Furthermore the helpfulness of my nonviolent effort is far far greater than I am able to appreciate until I have experienced it my self. My very own unique American patriot, Martin Luther King, points up this truth:

It is not overlooking the limitations of nonviolence and the distance we have yet to go to point out the remarkable record of achievements that have already come through nonviolent action. The 1960 sit-ins desegregated lunch counters in more than 150 cities within a year. The 1961 Freedom Rides put an end to segregation in interstate travel. The 1956 bus boycott in Montgomery, Alabama, ended segregation on the buses not only of that city but of practically every city of the South. The 1963 Birmingham movement and the climactic March on Washington won passage of the most powerful civil rights law in a century. The 1965 Selma movement brought enactment of the Voting Rights Law. Our nonviolent marches in Chicago last summer brought about a housing agreement, which, if implemented, will be the strongest step toward open housing taken in any city in the nation.

AMERICAN POLICE AUTHORITY

"The dogmas of the quiet past are inadequate to the stormy present.
The occasion is piled high with difficulty, and we must rise with the
occasion. As our case is new, so we must think anew and act anew.
We must disenthrall ourselves."

Abraham Lincoln

The briefest history of every citizen's police movement may
be allowed here. Police control derives from the inherent responsibility of the State official to legislate for the health, safety and
morals of his community. It is subject to the 14th Amendment
of my United States Constitution which specifies that no State
official shall deprive any person of life, liberty or property without due process of law. Police service *has* steadily broadened,
and it *is* increasingly difficult to chart its scope. One thing sure,
respect for the dignity of human individuality is easiest to conceive and proclaim by the sage statesman in the hallowed hall of
American justice, and hardest to honor and maintain by the
harassed policeman on the perilous highways of American
traffic. A lapse of the latter into any resort to any kind or degree
of civil disobedience, is hardly ever appreciated as understandable by his fellow citizen.

My police power is the executive civil force of my community
for maintaining everyone's safety and order. It is used to stop or
arrest my liberty only when it is best for me (whether I can
acknowledge the curb as best at the time or not). Historic police
work is of high antiquity, reaching back into early Egyptian
record. According to educated estimate, one of every twenty-
two of the people of 19th century England was a "criminal." It
was understandable therefore that the police organization by Sir
Robert Peel in 1829 first encountered much opposition. This
establishment of policemen, generally known as "Bobbies"
from Peel's first name, succeeded and subsequent metropolitan
police systems have been based on it. In my United States,
police work originated in colonial days; in townships in the
office of constable; in cities in the office of the night watch and

85

day-ward (later consolidated). In 1856 in the cities of New York and Philadelphia, standard police uniforms were adopted. The development of municipal police departments has been the issue of much experimentation, particularly with respect to administrative control. Since 1895 the Civil Service principle has proved widely helpful.

Effective law enforcement in every city, exceedingly complex, cannot be learned from textbooks. How to make it possible for the policeman to protect himself and to understand that only he *can* respect himself, are issues calling for continuing study in every effort to set up workable "police-community" activities. High-level exertion of the responsible citizen to see his personal identity in all of his "pecking order" is the most effective answer to the extremist activities of the irresponsible one. However it is the purpose of a "pecking order" to presume distinction between individuals. Ethnopsychological scholar Lévy-Bruhl recorded, "The more deeply the investigator probes the mentality of primitives or the semi-civilized, the more strongly is he impressed with the part which hierarchy plays in their lives."

It is ideal and practical patriotism whenever a civilian sees his police officer as his deeply respected official of his country's proud and honorable government. It is similarly helpful when each peace officer carries this same kind of dignified appreciation for the civic status of his every American citizen. All that *can* help officer and civilian alike to live each other respectfully is the *self* respect each one upholds. On account of the citizen's valiant efforts to overcome the difficulty of his limited self respect, there now appear civic trends in *this* direction of his getting the kind of governmental representation he asks for and elects. My chronic lax interpretation of the high ideals of my American Government leads to my every kind of disrespect for law and order, the essential guardians of my person's health.

A lady, or gentleman, has been well defined as one who can disagree agreeably. Little wonder if the metropolitan police officer feels "segregated," he and his fellow officers a wanted and unwanted "minority," since he must work mostly either with a stranger or with a scarcely known "law-breaker," either of whom may object violently to police interference, while the peace officer is only trying to do his required duty. The arresting officer's hardest and most helpful responsibility is that of keeping his own self respect (appreciation for his own individuality) while everyone around him seems to be losing that exclusive source of sanity.

The policeman, like the physician, cannot live a sheltered life. Unlike the physician, he must rely often upon reflex action. A great part of his work is emergency work for which there can be little or no preparation. Every arrest is potentially a delicate, dangerous operation. Citizen interference in it heightens the danger tremendously. Rarely can this experience be a constructive educational one on account of the painful emotions involved. It is defensible to use only the force absolutely necessary to restore responsible lifesaving order.

Wisdom of his civic living best enters into the youngest child's self development, then to be furthered by his elementary and later schooling, *without interval* throughout his life's course, as most precious self knowledge. The one and only source of sanity, as of insanity, is *in* each individual. This fact is the insight of insights. From earliest childhood on, the citizen needs to be able to *see for himself in himself* his lifesaving advantages in continuously studying and practicing his moral law of just self government. Calling attention to the uniquely self helpful Declaration of Independence in 1771, John Hancock observed, "It is highly proper that the memory of that Transaction, together with the causes that gave Rise to it, should be preserved in the most careful Manner that can be devised." Painful though it is to consider, I have had copious opportunity to observe how difficultly I have developed any of my appreciation for my personal identity. I see how I "found my mind" in my infanthood and childhood only to a greatly limited degree and how I have also had to work hard to open further this mind's eye of mine ever since then.

As an American citizen I have been accumulating a personal debt of moral obligation to my national truth of self sovereignty, to my ideal of supreme reverence for the worth of human *individuality*. Like every other citizen now being pressed for at least partial payment of this debt I need self education even to appreciate the fact that I owe myself this obligation. Right now as ever with specific respect to each American's heavy responsibility to *educate* himself to the self benefits of his so-called "racial integration," the real range of human individuality that includes its world, must be spelled out as often before. Thus America's all-time great scholar, Ralph Waldo Emerson, awoke, "Union is within . . . . Union must be ideal in actual individualism."

American freedom means my opportunity to learn that American government is my cherished *self* government,—not a benefit derived from outside of my self. Only my own unnoticed shortcoming *can* make me think I can be critical of my fellowman, white or black. My intolerance is my warning that I am unready to love my self wherever I feel the intolerance. However this kind of self understanding is hard to build up,—hence all of the get-free-quick, and "you free me," symptoms of limited self understanding in white and black man alike. *Violence is my ready substitute for unready conscious self education.* In 1775 John Adams tried to relieve his many civic frustrations by likening his country to "a great, unwieldy body. Its progress must be slow. It is like a large fleet sailing under convoy. The fleetest sailors must wait for the dullest and slowest. Like a coach and six, the swiftest horses must be slackened, and the slowest quickened, that all may keep an even pace." True enough, self experience is my only teacher but, as philosopher Kuno Fischer good naturedly remarked, Experience consists specifically in the living of what one does not wish to experience. I never want to acknowledge as my personal identity any of my self experience, if I feel more comfortable by disowning it.

From my limited experience I try to represent fairly my policeman's civic rights. I readily imagine the risks he takes in donning the uniform, wearing the badge, and above all carrying the gun. I understand the great concern as well as pride of each member of his family. I see the astonishing range of his emergency services as he confronts "the present moment and the troubled surface"* of his city. On every "call" he is on target. There is no rule-of-thumb wherewith he can rule out danger of every degree. There is no generality with which he can easily

*Walter Lippman

discharge his official problems. Every situation is a uniquely new one. He is strictly "on his own" and must make out the best way he can with what meager resources he has available. In crises seldom can he enjoy any relieving self enlightenment of insight. He is strengthened indeed if he has already learned that anger can only beget anger, aggression can only beget aggression, intolerance can only beget intolerance, quite as kindness must beget kindness, endurance must beget endurance, reverence for life must beget reverence for life, and so on. I know something of the innumerable temptations he must renounce and of the innumerable risks he must take. He may or may not know that dishonesty is always actually unhealthy, that there simply is no way for him to practice his governmental office dishonestly without having this self disrespect manifest itself in impairment of his body's health (stomach trouble, headaches, and so on) as well as in disorders in his life generally (wife trouble, child trouble, and similar heart aches).

I know something of my peace officer's experiences with his politicians, his often frustrating days "in court," his many other extra calls, and his inadequately remunerated system of 24 hour-a-day duty. And I admire him as an unsung patriot, quite as I appreciate the civic contribution made by each member of his family. The policeman potentially is good-will ambassador for the citizen and his city government. His performance can help to "make" his Commissioner, his Mayor, his City Council member, or his Civilian Fellowman. Everyone may well consider the inestimable value of the decent, kindly, honest, heedful, strong and healthy police officer for "good government." Ignorance, intolerance, incompetence, or superiority, cannot fit his high office. Authoritarian arrogance, rather than authentic obedience to his orders, may prove his most hazardous professional liability. His regular tour of duty is one of supreme concern for life, of guardian of property, of hard thinking, and of resolute stand.

Being a psychiatrist I wish to specify what I mean by the "mental health" of the Government official. For a brief description of the nature of a sound mind, I know of none saner than that which Thomas Jefferson wrote to Dr. Benjamin Rush, cosigner of the Declaration of Independence and father of American psychiatry. He listed the following qualities of the mind, in the order of their biological importance for him:

1. Good nature
2. Integrity
3. Industry
4. Science.

Insightful Mr. Jefferson evidently saw that by kindhearted cheer (good nature) he could succeed in continuously acknowledging his life experience as being entirely and only his own. Thus he scored the joy of living as of primary importance. Next, he observed that by recognizing his learning as biological, as made up merely and mightily of his own living, he could respect the wholeness of his being (integrity). Thus he scored *appreciated* individuality as of basic meaning for health. Then he noted that the man really "works" who can enjoy exercising his satisfying capacities for functioning (industry). Thus he scored the pleasure in willing service. He placed last the so-called knowledge of facts (science), thereby indicating that a man who enjoys applying himself, readily develops his capacities for self understanding ("knowledge of *his* world"). Thus he scored the truth that conscious will power develops in direct proportion to the development of heeded self knowledge, quite as involuntary behavior develops in direct proportion to unheeded self knowledge.

Hurry-up schemes and pressures to restore civic conditions as they used to be, or ought to be, or must become, are not wanting. Get-peace-quick notions fly back and forth, civilian trial boards, civilian policing measures, area crime groups, civil crime units, rumors of organized guerilla tactics, and so on. Meanwhile, it is wise to consider the dangerous philosophy of police work underlying such fragmentations of organized governmental functions.

An American citizen, I may tend to assume that I am ready to be a law unto my self, long before I have worked up my due sense of personal responsibility, inherent in every privilege of my

American citizenship. Therefore I may be peculiarly resentful of any imposition of authority seemingly "from without," of any curb to my acting uncivilly even while claiming my self capable of adequate self rule.

Many a veteran on the Force can tell how his experience has brought understanding and pacifying self confidence in his chosen field; how he has found ways of controlling his temper and of developing a peacemaking professional know-how with even the expert "troublemaker," the scofflaw. Basic friendliness from the side of able law-abiding members of the community-at-large, as well as from the members of the Police Department, treats the real source of policeman-civilian problems. Surely nothing can defeat effective police work faster than the civilian's picturing his own police corps as a foreign army in his midst.

Hence all the biological wisdom in my cultivating a liking for hard study of the nature of my mind. The expression "normal mental health" accurately refers to an established norm, rule or principle of ideal living that somewhat vaguely implies desirable, understandable, "socially acceptable," generally agreeable human behavior. Rarely if ever is the adjective "insightful" upheld as prerequisite to it, but the truth is that "insight" is the very unit of any kind of "mental health." I cannot safely spare my self the labor of shaping my mind to recognize that it can only observe its self, for exactly to the extent that I am heedful that my mentality is all and only about its self (regardless of how it may "seem" to be about somebody or something else) can I live myself insightfully. Insight is conscious self sight. Too much cannot be made over the insightful qualification called "willing consent." Jefferson recognized, "What has been the effect of coercion? To make one-half of the world fools and the other half hypocrites."

I may consider my governmental ideals and regulations as too demanding, and am free to help my self, *through due process of law,* to establish workable ideals and restrictions. Every instance of my civil disobedience must be observed as lawlessness calling for my subjecting my self to my "due process of law."

I find that I do not so much "solve" my difficult life problems as get over them somehow, survive them, grow wise by living through them. My responsible way out of my hardship, is through it. Thus, I can learn to use my "shortcomings." The blindness of my own preconceived opinions helps me to understand my fellowman's "blindness." Prejudices are not just simply airy ideas. They are habits, and a habit is a fixed mental condition which is renounced with difficulty always. Painful sensations and emotions are always associated with my giving up a mental attitude which I have held long enough so that I am addicted to it. However, courage itself is made up of trying what I am afraid to try.

The American reality of self sovereignty has been described as the "American dream" because it embodies this wonderful wish for the welfare of one's humanity: *Becoming a full grown responsible American is the most difficult of all civic achievements. It is best acknowledged that arduous evident self development underlies its attainment.* No amount of "received" courses in civics, or formal education of any kind or quantity, can produce acknowledgeable self responsibility. These statements bear much repeating.

My growth in citizenship, as all growth of mental maturity, may be described as learning to like experience which I formerly could only dislike. Thus, it is my citizenship development to get over feeling "better" or "worse" than my fellowman. I *am* my fellowman, and my awareness for that truth makes "comparison" obviously impossible. This fact of my comprehensive self identity is not advisably shaded or concealed, out of consideration for the pet prejudice of the mind not yet strong enough to create it for itself. If as an educator I gloss over this reality of American citizenship because it may seem disagreeable to the "many," I may well question my own devotion to it.

I must find in my self the willingness to endure preacefully the limited self helpfulness of my fellowman (his short temper, cutting sarcasm, or whatever). I must practice defensive "widespan" vision (driving my car, or walking my area, seemingly "for my other fellow"). For deliberately undergoing this kind of ordeal I help my self by possessing my President John F. Kennedy's immortal ideal, "We shall pay any price, bear any burden, meet any hardship, support any friend, oppose any foe, to assure the survival and the success of liberty." In his *"Resistance to Civil Government* Thoreau verses:

> I am too high-born to be propertied,
> To be a secondary at control,
> Or useful serving-man and instrument
> To any sovereign state throughout the world.

Most of all a peace officer needs to free his creative imagination for realizing: *there are always facts of life constantly underlying and fully explicating the strangest, most objectionable, and even extreme lawbreaking, kind of behavior.* His community, country or world, is unified now as never before. The onrush of human individuality necessitates forced growth of self tolerance, forced extension of self responsibility, forced appreciation for that supreme truth: the individuality (wholeness allness and unity) of the individual. Every such "forced" development is also *self* growth. Ideally there can be no real conflict of interest between a civilian and *his* policeman or *his* "city hall." My city police corps is best evaluated as my local "peace corps."

The following peacemaker orientation is merely an earnestly interested citizen's attempt to create for his own use a safe concept of a hard-working civilian. He serves his community's, his very own, interests most ideally and practically who may keep willing to try to:

Acknowledge reverence for human life in terms of his own, and temper his heroism and concept of duty with proper safety precaution. Let his fellowman see him saving and duly sparing his own life, let him behold a man who cares enough for his own life.

Observe lessons of his experience in cultivating nonviolent tolerant good nature as the only effective force for reducing irresponsible violent and impulsive behavior.

Value his professional identity as peacemaker, the sanest and safest conception of it. As John Stuart Mill defined his own mental power, "The test of a good mind is agreeing in the opinions of small minds."

Recognize that his peace officer has volunteered for a most critical government post, namely that of a persevering official peacemaker controlling government on his country's home front where there are, and are to be expected, constantly recurring instances of "lawlessness." Without freedom to learn even through such troublesome human behavior, the citizen cannot learn to govern his self responsibly.

Understand that living a human life peacefully is a most difficult accomplishment, regardless of how easy it sometimes may seem. Everyone is his whole world to his self.

Realize that his every fellow citizen when arrested or even "stopped," is always already suffering from overexertion, overwhelming life concerns, upsetting mental conditions, "more than he can take care of."

Work with the insight that every kind and degree of lawbreaking is *always* a painful symptom, an unenlightened shortsighted view of self help.

See his fellow citizen of every race, color and creed as vitally meaningful in his own life, deserving of all of the careful and caring attention he can summon. All that can dispel my delusion "racism" is my demonstrable truth *individualism.*

Know that his demonstration of authority seems often a hateful rather than kindly reminder of a parental or even marital yoke, and that any sign of authoritarianism (arrogance) is almost surely to be violently resented.

Renounce his innumerable temptations to wield his sovereign power at the cost of his self respect. My punitive attitude is always a grave deterrent to my effective law enforcement.

Identify his self with (feel equal to) his fellowman in trouble of any kind or degree, sufficiently to represent his protection, and if necessary his defense, while taking charge of him.

Appreciate that his identity as American citizen commits him to devoting his self steadfastly and longsufferingly to studying his ways for making his democracy work.

Function officially only as a peace force, insofar as possible "taking all sides" in order to *initiate due process of law.* It is specifically this very legal process that is every American's most prized and cherished governmental device.

AMERICAN CIVIL DISOBEDIENCE

"The organized charity, scrimped and iced,
In the name of a cautious, statistical Christ."
John Boyle O'Reilly

My greatest need of all regularly consists of my awakening to
new views of *self help,* new ideas about my own life's power, new
perspectives about the potential conduct of my mind. I am most
thankful for my insight: All of my help must be self help. I heed
my Henry L. Stimson's warning (1947) "No private program
and no public policy, in any section of our national life, can now
escape from the compelling fact that if it is not framed with reference to the world, it is framed with perfect futility." I can
discover no "private program" or "public policy" of meaning
for me except that which my own mind creates of my world of
my self. *This self orientation is indispensable for my understanding that my government cannot function as my "external
help."*
My most widespread of all American civil disobedience is
carried on unconsciously in the form of ignorance and disregard
for the one meaning: conscious self government. Like Diogenes
in search of an honest man, I encounter greatest difficulty in
finding my self consistently sticking to the hard task of making
my individuality into a responsible authority, capable of declaring and voluntarily fulfilling my American independence.
"What is the use of being elected or re-elected, unless you
stand for something?" Grover Cleveland asked. As has my fellow citizen, I have held many an office never knowing just what
I did stand for, until I developed sufficient strength of mind to
realize that I can and must stand for my own American way
of life,—*conscious* self government. Hence this little volume
focuses itself upon my problem of waking up *fully,* not merely to
"*the* times," or "*the* economy," or even to "*the* desperate situation of *the* Republic," but rather *to my whole self that includes*

and gives all of the meaning to any of my "the" this or "the" that.

In his final 1968 report to his House of Delegates as President of the American Medical Association Milford O. Rouse, M.D. stated, "We must consider responsibilities greater than those we have as physicians, by seeking ways to discharge our obligations as citizens. Physicians and their wives have the privilege and the responsibility of being active participating citizens in the communities where they reside. This includes the realm of political activity." If I do not recognize and discharge my political responsibility, does this neglect border on my civil disobedience with respect to my civil right?

Each of my American civil liberties serves my vital private interests, and hence I regard it as essential to my republican form of government. Without each of these freedoms, my *conscious* self sovereignty would suffer severely. All of my civil disobedience, quite as my civil obedience, is aimed at helping me to assert my independence. As awareness for my personal identtity extends itself to include more and more of my real world of self, my resort to civil disobedience becomes less and less. All of my civil obedience is the result of my learning from conscious self experience the law of how to get along with my self, how to live and love *all* of my self *as* my self. Every civil right of mine needs most loving protection, for it is evident to me that it is ever in terrible danger of seeming suspended or even revoked.

"Internal subversion" can never be a formidable threat to my American Constitution as long as its heart and soul, respect for the dignity and realization of the true extent of human individuality, remain in force and are revered for their appreciating all human life. However, due reverence for the true worth, the full measure, of human individuality comes dear. Even "We the people" is not always understandable as meaning "I the individual." "Safety from external danger" may become my most powerful and deadly distracter of my due concern for "Safety from internal danger." In the eighth *Federalist Paper,* about safety from external danger, Alexander Hamilton warns, "Even the ardent love of liberty will after a time give way to its dictates."

What my nation needs now more than any other kind of force is each individual's *conscious self power*. Can my realistic political action be taken on any one of my innumerable American fronts, such as fair housing or fair hiring or fair whatever, except to the extent that I can work on all of it where it is really taking place, specifically, in my very own world of my self? My creating a question accurately indicates my readiness to create its answer. Every citizen's exciting his mind to the awareness for his real greatness is necessary before he can see for his self that his self domination is his one and only possible, and wholly desirable, American mental development. Every access of conscious self identity provides me with further understanding of my nature based upon both deepening appreciation for my organic wholeness and widening responsibility for my political existence.

Invariably my deliberate civil disobedience is traceable to my assuming that my civil liberty should somehow allow me freedom in my "relationship" with my fellowman, in my so-called "external surroundings," rather than entirely in my living of my acknowledgeable self. This kind of self disorientation is always traceable to my inability to claim as my own, some of my living that I associate with my feeling of dislike. I find that my admitted civil disobedience is always a consequence of my inability to see that *all* of my living must occur completely within my own personal being. *Whenever I disown any of my mental power, I force my self to "reason" about it, since I cannot be conscious for it.* My dependence upon more or less violent reasoning or argument to arrive at truth occurs whenever my point of view is not one of conscious self observation that reveals to me clearly my only truth, the truth of my being. Following all of my clinical experience, my primary diagnosis of my fellowman is always the same one: *My patient is I.*

And now I record a mental power of the very greatest helpfulness to me in my efforts to sustain my life's tribulations and, at the same time, realize that my marvelous human individuality is really wonderful. I refer to keeping ready access to the free use of my imaginative power with which I produce my world of my mind. Constructive functioning of this creative energy is my source of my fundamental appreciation for my life itself. It is indispensable to the fine art of living consciously. I observe how my courage in daring to adventure with my power of creative imagination is helpful in my seeing all of my so-called "race rioting," or whatever I live, as being all and only my own. Furthermore, I observe how my uncontrollable frustration and my desperate uncontrollable violence associated with it stem from my neglecting and ignoring my truth that I *am* my creator of my family, neighborhood, nation, and world of my self.

I may legitimately live all of the painful feelings, and thoughts of self oppression natural to it, as intensely as necessary whenever I wish, provided that I can *imagine* each freely, and thus succeed in remaining consciously self contained with it. I may legitimately break every law of my land, only provided that I see all of my "law breaking" as my self controlled and self contained functioning of my imagination. Indeed such a self satisfying use of my imagination proves helpful as a safe expression for any and all of my momentary violent life dissatisfaction, as well as for my every wish for gratifying my self. Therefore I cannot repeat to my self too often: To the extent, and only to the extent, that this entirely safe and sane device of self can be understood as conscious mental freedom by my duly elected civic representative, and thus turned to his own self democratic use, I may continue to count heavily upon the prospect of enjoying further my legalized individual liberty.

Self education is required to produce the anarchist, communist, despot, quite as to produce the person capable of responsible self government. Therefore it is self learning of a very special order that is needed for the American citizen. *That order is no secret.* It is learning, every element of which is understood by teacher and pupil as nothing but each one's very own aroused mental potential. It is my awakening to the nature and needs of my very own human being only. It is my progress in discovering the truly wonderful *worldfulness* of my human life. It is my learning the lifesaving and life-giving benefit in my carefully cultivating most extensive altruism in my unique creaturehood, so that I can awaken to my self sufficiently to see that a benefit to anyone of my world is a benefit to me.

Realizing the crucial importance for my life in my discovering, claiming and constantly exciting my sense of personal identity in *all* of my living, I persevere in the practice of this conscious way of life. I am my only seeming "invisible man," and there are innumerable temptations besetting me to try to lose sight of my self. My Ralph Ellison's soulful odyssey, *The Invisible Man,** stirs up my inmost being by revealing how torture can compel and combat divine man's focusing his interest in the abiding truth of his own identity. As did Destutt de Tracy, so William James pointed out: "Individuality is founded in feeling; and the recesses of feeling, the darker, blinder strata of character, are the only places in the world in which to catch real fact in the making."

The free use of creative imagination in no way obstructs but rather facilitates all other valuable mental functioning. It is cultivated by every artist as precious life force. As a child, I doubt if I could have gone on living without it. As a man, I find I need and use it as much as ever. Without it, the significance of my great minded concept, *self fulfillment,* lacks its most precious meaning. With it, my most valued life orientation, self consciousness, permits my observing the full scope of my whole creaturehood. During my turbulent adolescent living I restrained much of my creative imagination with shame; during my developing my conscious self identity I have restored that sanity saving vitality with pride. I now see that my rejection of, or unbelief for, any idea or meaning whatever of mine, has its only source in my threatened conscious self tolerance or love. It is natural for my self love to protect itself from further development or alteration stress by warding it off with feelings of dislike or unhappiness of some specific quality. My current limit of self love also serves as the boundary of my ability to acknowledge my self identity. All of my self violence is perpetrated anonymously since I do not recognize that it is my self I am hurting.

Whenever from desperation over the inadequacy of all else I decide upon a course of civil disobedience, hoping to focus attention upon the desirability of changing a law that seems to run counter to my natural constitution, I must expect and be pre-

*Random House, Inc., New York, 10022, 1947

pared for the due process of law that currently obtains. This may mean my arrest and temporary imprisonment. It is least objectionable but most effective for my illegal action to be consistently nonviolent. Quite as Gandhi viewed the efficacy of nonviolence for direct action: "It is not one form, it is the only form." In his essay, *Resistance To Civil Government,* a favorite of Ghandi, Thoreau declares, "Under a government which imprisons any unjustly, the true place for a just man is also a prison."

My apparent nonviolence cannot mean that I do not care, or that I am feelingless, or that I do not suffer. Quite the contrary, I mean by it, my enduring violent feelings but with the composure appropriate to my recognizable self continence. My uncontrollable feelings of violence and the thoughts corresponding to them are biological necessities whenever I feel overwhelmed by hurt. Such extreme tension, always involuntary, is my helpful form of my crying out, "Ouch, I hurt all over!"

My any and every attempt to account for anything human in terms of more than one human mind (my own) is doomed to absolute illusion from the start. This is my primary scientific law. Obedience to it saves me from claiming I can somehow "go out of my mind," or that I can somehow experience more than what my own living creates.

In *Time and Free Will,* Henri Louis Bergson observes, "Probably animals do not picture to themselves, beside their sensations, as we do, an external world quite distinct from themselves." Sigmund Freud studied his mind's need to avoid overwhelming itself with conscious responsibility for its creating its own world, and how it helped itself to escape its painful realization by disowning it in the name of somebody or someone else. He pointed out how his mind tended to disclaim or ignore responsibility for its experience whenever this attempted self rejection might result in relief of intolerable tension.

In any event, when I lose sight of the truth of my own self experience I substitute some of my living I am not recognizing as my own. Then my recovering my conscious self sight is of the nature of my again feeling the quick of it. My thus becoming sensitive again for it spares me from injuring my self with it through uncontrolled violence.

I explain nonviolent resistance or protest or aggression somewhat as the individual's conscious effort towards self contained expression of his painful emotional tensions while undergoing the ordeal of trying to extend or keep from extending his egoism's growing into its "altruism."

Strategy of nonviolent action is important as every person's pacific activist orientation to problems arising from his efforts to "socialize" his individuality, by acknowledging *his* fellowman in his estimate of his personal identity. As all else seemingly inhuman, it is entirely a helpful product of my individual mind designed to provide respect for obstinate facts of my limited self tolerance while I am undergoing the process of enlarging my conscious self realization. It is most helpful if I conduct my confrontations with *my* very own fellowman with insight that 1) all of the experience is personally mine, 2) I cannot function irresponsibly in this self confrontation without hurting my self, and 3) I must experience the whole of the action as my own activity in order to observe that much of my self completely. This practice suggests Lincoln's wide-open broad mindedness in describing honesty as the willingness to "take all sides" of a problem in order to examine it fairly.

Ideal nonviolent method allows opportunity for each individual to find sufficient facts to warrant his acknowledging his personal identity in his so-called "adversary." There can be no argument or dispute where each person can realize that 1) all of his views must be only about his self and 2) there is no possibility therefore that he and his fellowman might be talking on the same subject. Clearly this degree of self responsibility is most difficult to achieve, and then most difficult to have accessible when most needed. Hence all of the hot disputation regularly leading to self destruction of some degree. Self perceptive Charles D. Aring, M.D., delivers a strong glow for good government,

> The formalism of trials, oriented toward simplification, works contrary to the extraordinary complexities of human behavior. Often,

even with all the evidence that can be derived by any and every technique, there may be no answer reducible to a simplistic "yes" or "no." . . . . The adversary system was begun in an uncomplicated society to preserve the rights of the people. In a social system where complexities have increased exponentially, the anachronisms become apparent.

AMERICAN DIPLOMACY

"It really hurts me very much to suppose that I have wronged anybody on earth."

Abraham Lincoln

Every American citizen may comfort himself considerably regarding the potential helpfulness of his professional democratic diplomat by reading Henry M. Wriston's interesting little book, *"Diplomacy in a Democracy."** The American diplomat, whose mind is disciplined in sensing his identity in his fellowman, has the most powerful means of understanding that is possible. It is this kind of readiness for world citizenship which is the most urgent need of my world today. As Abraham Lincoln said, the Declaration of Independence "gave liberty not alone to the people of this country, but hope to all the world, for all future time."

The great seal of the United States carries in Latin the motto: *a new order of the world.* The American diplomat who has trained his mind to observe that his world is his own, and that his every fellowman's world is *his* own, has in mind the program for peace through this wisdom of self appreciation. The cure for each complaint about democracy ever continues to be more democracy. The conversion of "They" and "We" into "I" epitomizes democratic diplomacy. It is noteworthy that the communist speaker or writer must patriotically favor "We" instead of "I"; or "Ours" instead of "Mine."

As Dwight D. Eisenhower observed, "The great struggle of our times is for the hearts and souls of men—their very inmost souls. If we are going to be strong we must be strong in spirit. . . . We must be devoted with all our heart to the values we defend. We must know that each of these values and virtues applies with equal force at the ends of the earth and in our relations with our neighbors next door."

American poet and diplomat James Russell Lowell recorded,

*Harper & Brothers, New York, 1956.

"It is by presence of mind in untried emergencies, that the native metal of a man is tested." Presence of mind is founded only upon self consciousness. The illusion "relativity" is the product of negation of individuality. Such is the kind of political insight enjoyed by Adam Smith, James Mill, Jeremy Bentham, and many another self reliant independent: "The pursuit of individual advantage is admirably connected with the universal good of the whole." Thomas Hill Green also said it well, "The self is a social self." And ancient Solon knew, "That is the most perfect government under which a wrong to the humblest is an affront to all."

War is the issue of declared irresponsibility created by negated individuality. Thus every war has been over the control of "property" unrecognized as self property. Machiavelli accounted for war accurately as the State's (nobody's) prerogative in its right to preserve and augment its power. The locus of state sovereignty is nowhere, a most difficult place to find for the fixing of responsibility. Equipped with this insight, the American diplomat is most effective as an ambassodor of peace and good will. Self consciousness confers the needed talent and tact of statesmanship.

I can have but one possible government, namely my own. However it must be either conscious self government of democracy or unconscious self government of dictatorship. Diplomatic expediency may, and often does, require understanding endurance of one's wish to have everyone of his world immediately begin to enjoy the self benefits of democratizing his living, every individual's democratization being a life process which may immediately begin but must grow from within only. William Benton wisely observes: "Politics is the most vital of the human arts. It is an art that has to be learned. And it is a difficult art. Einstein said, 'Politics is more difficult than physics.' You will certainly agree with Einstein that our world is more likely to die of bad politics than of bad physics."

My "learning politics" involves my awakening to my realization that *all* disputation is empty of sanity. Each disputant is necessarily always talking exclusively to his self, and as a rule without listening to what he says, but fully expecting his opponent to be able to do his listening for him. Might as well expect his opponent to be able to do his talking for him, also. In his *Republic* Plato creates his view that dialectic be studied only by the person twenty-five or over, for he would then be less likely to use the device for quarrelsome argument.

Just by beholding only my self in my politics, can I attain the sane view that my art and science of government must exist in me, and not the converse. My science of my mind is based upon my self observation, and I create my every self observation.

Grover Cleveland

MY AMERICAN GOVERNMENT AND
MY RELIGIOUS LIBERTY

"We have solved by fair experiment the great and interesting question whether freedom of religion is compatible with order in government, and obedience to the laws. And we have experienced the quiet as well as the comfort which results from leaving every one to profess freely and openly those principles of religion which are the inductions of his own reason, and the serious convictions of his own inquiries."

Thomas Jefferson

Each of my American forefathers who instituted a new order in the world, then known as the will of the people to honor the will of every citizen, was awake to the fact that human nature occurs only in the form of individual human being. Each of these consciously great minded lawmakers saw clearly that human individuality is a unique, subjective, mind forming, spirited, soul. And each one recognized the need to establish government compatible with the spiritual or religious nature and needs of his every citizen. Each sought a self government reconcilable with his attaining appreciation for his own divinity.

My discipline of my will to live sanely, derived only from my arduously earned self consciousness, has enabled my concentration of my self to *heeding* my unified identity in all of my experience, that is, in all of my meaningful living. Sustained devotion to *conscious* self orientation reveals me to my self as savior of the meaning of my life. This degree of responsibility and appreciation for my living, makes personally relevant my attributes of power and glory I formerly ascribed to a divinity I could not then identify fully as entirely my own creation. I am my own redeemer as I resurrect any of my living I previously considered "not-I" and honor it as my personal existence only.

"The unexamined life is not worth living," said Socrates, according to Plato. The examination of my life had to be based upon insight that 1) I do the examining, and 2) I am the examined. Any and all of my consciously ignored or in any way denied individuality provides the basis for my necessary religious truth that I do not seem to be able to acknowledge as wholly created by my self for my self. However there *must* be my identity underlying whatever *I* assert is either mine or "not-mine." *There can be no so-called "object" of my mind that is not a process of my mind's subjectivity.* This clear view of my wholeness allness oneness and unity is of paramount scope for my finding and keeping the peace, since it reveals the locus of any and all of my human behavior as being entirely and only in my human individuality. My competent citizenship is a moral issue.

I can hold myself responsible *only* for any act or omission that I can observe *is* lived by me. Becoming admittedly responsible for all of my living through becoming aware that all of it *is* my own, is my definition of "growing up" in my American citizenship as an individual capable of keeping the peace. However, I trace much of my troubled living to my illusion that I can be somehow capable of more or less than my own functioning. To illustrate, I may indulge my illusion that I can use my mind to be able to have something to do with "somebody else," or to be able to have "somebody else" have something to do with me. Or I may imagine my "doing" to be some kind of exception to my *being,* so that I can appear to "do" something to "another" or to experience "another's doing" something to me. These illusions support major self deceptions such as my assuming the possibility of "interpersonal relations," or "intercommunication," or whatever "inter" this or "inter" that appearing to deny the intact integrity of my individuality.

It is only human nature for me 1) to fear the condition of my living my self as if I can be more or less than one individual and consequently 2) to observe my acknowledgeable self as if it could be opposed to my unacknowledgeable self. Such appearance of "conflict" is always traceable to trouble signalizing certain unrecognizable personal identity of mine. Seeing only my own being where I formerly could not acknowledge or recognize it, is always an heroic act of saving my life.

The science of man is based upon his conscious self observation. The self-sensible scientist systematically does the best he can to discover and honor his identity in his world. I too observe that I may be regarded as a political animal in view of my awareness of the benefit to my self in living my fellowman ethically. As I admittedly create in my self experiencing mind my meanings for my world, I can also discipline my self to recognize my fellowman as a complex of my unified identity, as a distinct individuation of my own individuality. Provided that my self consciousness can keep up with with my self growth, I soon awaken to the civic insight about the self helpfulness in constructing self governing contrivances to serve the ideal political condition occurring in my societal living.

The foundation upon which the American citizen's democratic testament rests cannot be safely assumed to be that of his very own rejected selfness, e.g., "the people," but must be located insightfully in his own declared individuality. As noted, each American citizen *is* all of his own "the people," but he must develop great strength of mind to be able to support this insight. He is his own "many" or "few" or whatever. I am my self, my whole self, and nothing but my self. My acknowledging that truth depends upon my disciplining my mental strength to be able to make that strenuous effort.

Thomas Jefferson discovered that only freely self willed growth of conscious self knowledge can cultivate the conscious self power essential for conscious self government. Every individual's political development is an expression of his life process which he must grow consciously or unconsciously from within his being. His "due process of law" is each citizen's own mental process.

For years now my intentional education work has consisted of my heedfully learning that my teachings are my life creations, my self developments. I have discovered the truth in my Thomas Jefferson's dictum, "Health is no more than learning." The corollary of that pronouncement is equally true: Endangered health (so-called "illness" or "injury") is also no more than learning. I must learn specific life lessons in order to develop my self in any way. To fulfill my greatness with awareness for it, my specific life lesson must be my discovering that my education is all and only my growth and specific cultivation of my own mind.

Whether I heed or ignore my true greatness, decides whether my conduct will be that becoming to a clearly all great, or to a seemingly mostly small, souled individual.

All of his "political language" is each citizen's uniquely own instrument of thought, labelled "politics." It required great exertion in self awareness for me to be able to renounce my superstition that I can "communicate with my fellowman by use of my language." My language is my wonderful self development (idiolect) for my securing and operating definitive views of my own abundance, having no more "communication" value than any other development of my inviolable individuality. The *real* function of my linguistics is to help me organize *my* life, direct *my* power, mind *my* own interests.

It is evident that for me to be an American citizen, other than merely by birth and name, I must be willing to work hard and steadily at it. My work-up of my insight that conscious individuality is the only possible "united humanity," or All-Real, or divine world plan, requires undivided, arduous and persevering conscious self devotion. I must awaken to my living as my consciously experiencing my personal identity, in all of my "burden of received knowledge," such as all of my vocabulary, all of my "commonly accepted opinion" or "argument," and every other unconscious self identity.

By merely accumulating my unconscious self identity I come as close to moral nihilism as is possible for me. My extension of my self consciousness is my only way of extending my self conscientiousness. Whatever I cannot live as my conscious personal identity, I cannot live as a conscious responsibility. Unselfish self activity constitutes self contradiction. William Gladstone worded it, "What is morally wrong cannot be politically right."

In his *Fountainheads of Freedom,** dedicated to John Dewey, philosopher of American democracy, life loving Irwin Edman noticed,

> What is cherished and what is cherishable in the democratic faith are
> best understood by seeing how the idea has lived and grown from the

*With the collaboration of Herbert W. Schneider, Reynal and Hitchcock, New York, 1941.

Old Testament prophets to the prophets of later ages, facing different problems, finding different formulas, but uttering essentially the same hope and ideal . . . . To be free means to be one's self . . . . Men from the beginning of history cherished individuality, but they have also been more than willing to barter the liberty of being different for the comfort of being like other men.

Declared Jefferson, "The care of human life and happiness is the only legitimate object of good government." The essence of my American citizenship is also that of my recognized ethic, namely full-measured appreciation br the complete sufficiency of my individuality. As already noted, the solipsistic life orientation can deny nothing, being the only self orientation which *can* and *must* consistently affirm all of its living by acknowledging it as its own. My practice of it demonstrates my necessity to extend my self consciousness if I would extend my good will and love.

My Jefferson consciously aimed at making his Declaration of Independence an "expression of the American mind." As David Hume said, the mere formulation of a problem is almost half of its solution. How can I explain my need for ethics, is a question of paramount importance vexing my religious dogmatist, freethinker, and every member of each Society for Ethical Culture, alike. My unitary conception of my world of my mind, based upon the biologically adequate extent of my conscious existence, fully and only accounts for all of my interest in being both just and loving ("good").

My mind's capacity to separate itself into divisions (for example, to permit classification, or to provide for concentrated study of its self in one direction or another) is a power I must use insightfully in order that I may not overlook my intact mental oneness and wholeness. Often I am tempted, beyond my resistance, to dissociate my mind into faculties or fractions, and overlook the truth that only my wholeness can function, only my individuality can constitute its every individuation. Madame de Stael prudently viewed this source of fearful danger, "To divide, in order to comprehend, is a sign of weakness in philosophy; as to divide, in order to rule, is a sign of weakness in political power."

111

It is helpful to illustrate just how my mind's diremptive power can be used by me unconsciously so that before I realize what is happening I can lose track of the truth of the perfection of my whole being. My "ethic" is a word, a name for my "science of values," referring to considerations of my "conscience." My need to use a conscience arises only when my whole mind first dissociates itself so that it can appear to me that what I mean by "conscience" seems set apart from the rest of my life's meaning. Resident in my conscience subdivision is my acknowledged perfection, the rest of me being adjudged by me as if "imperfect." Once I use my mind to deny *any* of its one-and-only value of perfection I immediately require my self to provide some other "value." This mental dissociation simultaneously involves my creating each of my compensatory meanings to function as an unconscious bridge from my self living I cannot acknowledge as perfect to that which I can. I refer to pejoration and melioration, as well as to "otherness," "plurality," "externality," and so on. Indispensable for my adequate self care is my clear recognition that all of me is good. If there be any "greatest good" it lies in my capacity for this precious recognition. Overlooking my holy ground of wholeness (oneness) in order to save what conscious mindedness I *can* acknowledge, I thus involve my self in endless argument based upon my imagined "duality" of my goodness and badness.

Hence it is that each ethicist carefully locates his ethic in the so-called "inner man." Leslie Stephen asserts "the clear enunciation of one principle. . . . characteristic of all great moral revelations. . . . may be briefly expressed in the phrase that *morality is internal.*" In his *Prolegomena to Ethics,* T. H. Green concentrates approval on this inner spring, "It is not by the outward form that we know what moral action is. We know it, so to speak, on the inner side." James Martineau introspects in his *Idiopsychological Ethics,* "We have another term still more expressive of the inward feeling characteristic of a moral being: there is, it seems, something that binds,—in Latin, *obliges* us,—puts a restraint on the direction of our will, yet not an outer restraint upon its power, but an inner restraint."

Yet on and on my ethicist magnanimously pays the enormous

cost of endless judging and reasoning to support his unconscious mental dissociations into seeming many-sidedness. Only by restoring my appreciation for my wholeness, by practicing the oneness inherent in my self consciousness, can I gradually learn to renounce my mind's habit of seeing double or multiple to any extent. There is no way for human individuality to multiply or divide itself, to make more or less than one out of one. By honoring this one truth I can practice ideal self preservation. This honor is the guardian of my morality, my willingness to observe and enjoy the allness of my self containing individuality. I find working at making this self estimate to be my most difficult and most rewarding form of self culture, my beholding in the mirror of my self that I am *all* and *only* whatever I can see.

Insight derived from observing that whatever is, is of necessity (i.e., *is* for sufficient accounting), equates perfection and reality, enabling me to feel my identity in my divinity simply by noticing its source and course in my mind. It is often too heady for me to heed that I am all that I *can* have any interest in, in my created world. It always helps me to realize that setting out from my mind (which moves ever in its own element), it is possible for me to account for whatever I live; but that setting out from any place but my mind, I cannot account for anything at all,—certainly not for my self. I understand Spinoza's assertion: Every individual thing, so far as in it lies, endeavors to persist in its own being.

My striving to feel my identity, to see that I am equal to myself, is my one source for the conscious equilibrium that enables me to prize justice, called by Aristotle, "the noblest among the virtues." The concluding proposition of Spinoza's *Ethics* comes to mind here, "Blessedness is not the reward of virtue but virtue itself."

In her spirited treatise, *Government Is Self Government,** devoutly mindful Margaret Laird legislates,

> An individualist is not one who lives for himSelf but is one who lives universally *within* himself as himSelf . . . As long as we look to Statesmen, to Peace Treaties, to United Nations to bring about what

*The Portal Press, Evanston, Illinois, 1952

Daring to persevere in recognizing my self *wherever* I formerly overlooked my self in my living is my only possible way for me to "renew contact with nature." My only living that "honors creation for its own sake" is living that I honor as being my own. I am my only "Great Society." My conscious meaning of my life can match the marvelous products of my labor only when I can recognize my personal identity in each product. My "domestic tranquillity" is my peace of mind. However as everyone else of my world, I tend to believe, "Give me the luxuries of life, and I can get along without the necessities."

Sustained consciousness for its own worth is what my mind requires in order to be quickened and renewed. But why should I ever overlook my very own tremendous mental power? Apparently quite as Sigmund Freud discovered, merely on account of its frequently being too astounding. My conscious mind, that is, my living of my mind which I can responsibly claim as my own, is able to endure only limited excitement in a given period. Whenever my living of excitation exceeds the mental tolerance which is adequate for my sense of personal identity, I suffer some degree of shock, am stunned "out of my wits," and lose the so-called "presence of mind" which I need for prizing my life's true extent. Inability to see all of my living as my own necessitates my imagining some other kind of substance than my self. Thus I force my self into indulging an illusion of "duality" at the expense of my appreciation for my real *unity*.

Nevertheless all of my truth can be realized only in my self. To imagine it as being outside of me is to imagine it as deprived of its only reality. An insightless notion of "externality" carries all of the intense conviction characteristic of any other delusion and produces a certainty of mind favorable to rigidity and consistency of compulsive action. Such "dead sure" imagining creates a disrelish for the vagueness and uncertainty often essential for appreciating the actual novelty of living.

No self heedlessness is fraught with greater irrationality than is my persistent disregard for the amazing providence of my own nature. Self ingratitude for one's own plenteous abundance, unfailing helpfulness, and continuous supply of all-giving life its self, is properly the source of most painful signs of mental neglect. Factually oriented, there can be no such possiblity as a poor man,—a seemingly self ungrateful one, yes. My mind's process of realizing its astonishing meaningfulness is my only source for my recognizing the immensity of the meaning of my life. That everyone, unaided, must create his own just conception of his true greatness in order to promote his highest welfare, is the open secret of the ideal "making of him." That everyone *unassisted* must come to his senses sufficiently to see that all that he admires or abjures is his own wonderfulness, is the most difficult of all of his life lessons. That each individual, *all and always alone,* must discover that he is *all* there is, and that this self insight is his only reliable tie to *his* fellowman,—such is his highest wisdom revealing the highest purpose of his existence. That every person's most rewarding life attainment, his *summum bonum,* specifically is *his most satisfying answer to the meaning of his being,* is both a religious and patriotic self orientation for each American citizen.

As does every convenient phantasy involving "duality," the artificial dichotomy of "private selfish affections" and "public social affections" requires costly compensation in that it obscures self conscious viewing of indivisible human selfhood. Such attempted setting up of a double life in one human constitution creates a self deception intolerable for human being, necessitating its resorting to symptom formation to live through it. Thus the ancient form of human sacrifice comes to life in the form of "self sacrifice for others," made to pass for biologically adequate self devotion.

Two concurrent and opposite courses of life are not possible for individual man, e.g., divine and human, or sacred and secular, or religious and scientific, or individualistic and social, or individualistic and neoplastic, and so on. My nature is infallible and indefectible and completely individual, despite all of the helpful faultfinding terms I often use to describe it. I have no choice, other than to be aware or unaware of my ever present divine nature. Perfection is always present everywhere, quite as individuality is. Its recognition in the form of full acknowledgment (of omnipresent individual perfection) is all that can be perfectly wanting. No experience is ever observed clearly until its complete excellence, its faultlessness, is fully appreciated.

My way of living my world constitutes for me my ideal ethic. With the insight that God is all, I may declare a "theft" is as much the will of God as is a "gift;" "cruelty" is as much God's will-being-done as "gentleness;" "gluttony" is as much divinely enforced as "temperance." Each so-called "sin" is as sanctified an action as any so-called "virtue," temporarily serving the "sinner's" self preservation ideally. In other words, all so-called unethical activity is my unrecognized ethical conduct. The health or perfection of soul life consists precisely in *whatever* way it exists. Complete study of the all-sufficing facts discovers every kind of human behavior as a "science of right conduct," as an expression of "the good will."

The self-evident self observation that individual self interest is the valid end of all action, is no mere "doctrine." Such "ethical egoism" is inevitable *reality*. The self disregarding notion that the actual and impelling motive of any self activity can be other than self interest contradicts itself.

Despite nearly every critic's allegation to the contrary, neither Hobbes nor Spinoza ignored his concept of the importance of his *species* in his personal ethic aimed strictly at his own self preservation. Neither one fell into that tender trap of considering his self merely as a dependent member of a species to which he owed his nature and existence. Only the individual consciously capable of supreme service to his self preservation can fully attest his devotion to *his* fellowman. No "species" of mankind was ever born or endowed with individual life, or provided with any system of self preservation whatsoever. All of the meaning of mankind exists only in the mind of the individual creating it. Furthermore I do not reproduce my self in my offspring. Every human being must do all of his creating of his self by his self.

The highest distinction of the insightful ethicist is that he recognizes the indissoluble unity of his mind as it goes on constituting its self of each and every meaning of his world. My individual human welfare is always and only my individual concern, and it consists not merely in the exercise, but specifically in the *conscious* exercise, of all of my self interests, of all of my potentially conscious *power*. I regard my self sovereignty as profoundly religious, in that its language is sacred poetry of and to me. Somewhat similarly Paul Elmer More and George Santayana considered poetry to be the natural language of religion.

The root of my conception of "otherness" lies in my infant mind's predilection to attribute little or no necessity to the importance of its *claiming* its original power of creating its world. "Otherness" involves illusion of a clear "separation" of self experience into acknowledgeable and unacknowledgeable personal identity. I help my self immensely by tracing my burdensome accumulation of unconscious (consciously denied) selfness to the incompleteness of my original primary appreciation for the real allness wholeness oneness and unity of my self.

Only when conscious self observation is the scientist's manner and matter of investigation can his full-measured appreciation for the inviolable wholeness of his human individuality be duly taken into account by him. His other scientific work effects the heat of personal emotion rather than the light of personal consciousness. Thus, Shaftesbury optimistically emphasizes the pleasing aspects of human nature. Hobbes pessimistically scores man's unhappy living. Understandable becomes Horace Walpole's judgement in his letter to Sir Horace Mann (1742), "The world is a comedy to those that think, a tragedy to those who feel."

Immanuel Kant said, the only task in one's ethic is to collect the commands of "duty" and arrange them under a universal formula. He could not reach this formalistic view at the cost of disregard for the nature and needs of his human individuality. Individuality worship just *seems* incompatible with the dictates of "common" morality. A person's first and only possible duty is to take care of his self the best way he momentarily can, until his experience adds to his stock of conscious self knowledge. *Only conscious self knowledge can carry any ethical responsibility.*

Whoever would "re-establish the rights of humanity" must accomplish this mission wholly and solely and consciously in his own individuality, the only place where any and all of his humanity can be found. Self perfection is no possible ethical goal, for it is omnipresent. Perfect awareness (self awareness) for all of my very own self perfection is my single possible ethical goal. Every individual rightly makes his moral law by and for his self, he rightly cannot make his self subject of anyone or anything of his own world.

Despite many a valiant effort to establish sanction for the positive standards of morality in some asserted self negation no one has ever been able to discover upon what foundation such "unselfishness" could rest, or from what source other than his own nature an individual's binding code of ideals or renunciations could derive its authority.

When I can see my sensations, perceptions, impulses, and experiences of every kind as surely mine, I cannot and do not complain of tyranny by an alien power (as if I could be "in" a delusion of alien influence or persecution or infidelity, or overpowered by "suggestion," "persuasion," and "seduction;" or exert "power over others;" and so on). In order to be able to *feel* free at will, I must have succeeded in living enough of my mind as really being mine to be able to use it at will. Attainment of such appreciation for the allness of my subjectivity is experienced as observable spiritual release, as the divinity of humanity, as a very personal so-called "mystic" event. "So-called," for every human experience is mystic in the metaphysical sense that it is based upon a subjectively incommunicable development in one individual.

With each access of *conscious* freedom the joy of living becomes clearly apparent. The experience of sensing one's freedom has been identified with religion, patriotism and other recognizable "inner" being, including psychotherapy. Greatest religious statements emphasize the individuality of individuality, namely, subjectivity, My religion is my putting my soul to sane use in honoring all of my self as the glory of God. My living is seen clearly while I see it as free, good, beautiful, true, helpful, unique, new, original, desirable, personal, and in every way ideal living.

As Tennyson divined, "self-reverence, self-knowledge, self-control" alone can "lead life to sovereign power." The spirit of this kind of insight well rules my self educational effort. What makes knowledge at all worth "having" is the fact that it is my *being*. Such is the wisdom bearing nature of all of my mental functioning. I am a scientist, not with the motivation that my findings may be translated into some far-reaching application eventually, but with my present realization that my researching is my culminating self development extending my helpfulness right now, revealing my precious self power immediately. I am religious, not with the motivation that my piety, my divinity affirmation, may be translated into usefulness "in the next world," but with my present realization that my study and practice of my spiritual power is my culminating ensouling of my individuality, revealing my precious godliness right now.

Whatever I live is I, is my self awakened ethical pronouncement. Seeing all of my dependency as self dependency is the full-measured view of my independence. Consciously subdued by to and for my own power, I can grow to appreciate my actual potency. Learning to deposit my experience in my I-bank, I cultivate courageous self insight of just proportion, that is, coterminous and identical with my heroic self world. Educating my mind with the full consciousness characteristic of love, I dare to become the awakened godsmith (Dryden) able to appreciate my godliness. The life of practiced self observation is replete with satisfying argument, all of it exalting my wonderfulness, all of it providing discipline in my appreciating my wholly human empire.

The mystery of divine providential government of man is solved completely by a thorough understanding of the role of *fact* in human experience. Reverence for the force of fact is whole-souled service in one's godly power. It is *evidently* godly to work one's perfection consciously. Presumably only man can discipline his mind to appreciate that the factors constituting his behavior sufficiently account for it as perfect creation. Every creature is the exact product of his own living, but the human creature alone can learn to *recognize* that only he can make his self perfectly in one way or another. As his recognized self consciousness varies, so does the amount or degree of his deliberate, purposeful shaping of his life.

My only *possible* wordly prosperity is that of my individual world; there being no other for me. Where respect for this fact (that all observation is self observation) prevails, it is possible for my so-called selfishness to become recognizable as unmistakable godliness. Advance in learning that my subjectivity *is* my all, attests my *responsibly* growing my human nature. Persevering conscious effort to extend the degree and range of my self consciousness ("self analysis") is uniquely human endeavor, *the ultimate in self discipline of the individual mind.*

Obviously even an animal must be only self oriented, self experiencing, self sensing, self perceiving, and so on. Also obviously, every human being must be only self conscious, for his own life is all that he *is* to experience. *The distinction is mighty: self consciousness is not at all the same as acknowledged self consciousness.*

SUMMARY VIEW

"Must a government, of necessity, be too strong for the liberties of its own people, or too weak to maintain its own existence?"

Abraham Lincoln

It has been my intention to speak of my American government as of my self. As I review what I have written, it is not about liberty, it *is* liberty, and I am grateful for my American being that makes it safe, sane and sacred.

An adequate *science of man* will begin to be written only when its author begins to work up an adequate appreciation for the meaning of his self identity, a clear insight into the one world of his individual mind. Only this comprehension for the *unity* of self identity can spare the author all of the phantom problems he creates in such chimerical dualities as "thou and I," "body-mind," "psyche and soma," "physical and mental," "neurological and psychiatric," "ideal and material," "objective and subjective." My *conscious* individuality, insightful self identity, precludes every kind of plurality and ambivalence or confusion.

I must take care not to distract my attention from the one point at issue: Does my individuality really consist only of individuality, or, Am I made up of my self plus some other element or elements? How can I even imagine anything that I am not? There can be no duality or plurality of any kind imaginable except that created by in and of my unified integrated *individual* mind. The importance of awareness for this truth cannot be overemphasized.

I must see to it that any subject created by my own mind, such as my imagined plurality, may not appear to be able to subject me to it, so that I may then seem to my self to be another than *one*. The kind of losing my awareness for my mental integrity, for my inviolable self identity, obtains in the world of my mind, unless I see to it that it does not. Quite as Samuel McChord Crothers soliloquized in his delightfully self conscious *The Gen-*

tle Reader, an author of any work will write better for having some knowledge of the subject on which he treats.

Biological truth of the very greatest lifesaving importance is the following rarely recognized one: I cannot see at all with my "physical" eyes, or hear at all with my "physical" ears, or touch at all with my "physical" body. It is my mind only which and with which I can sense, see, or hear, or otherwise experience (awaken) through my senses.

Without my mind I cannot sense anything in any way. With my mind my sensing becomes my power to awaken to my knowledge of my world of self. It is possible to use the terms "sense" and "meaning" interchangeably, provided that it is understood that each term names a distinctive *mental* construct or event, and that each term refers to its coiner or creator as its only possible subject matter. By sensing consciously I come to life consciously.

This meaningful sensing only with my mind, is all that provides any of the importance of whatever I do sense. It furnishes me with all of the visual or auditory or any other sensory experience I live. What can I be living but my very own self alone in any of my functioning? Asserts scientist Thomas Huxley in his *Helps to the Study of Berkeley:*

> It is undoubtedly true, then, of all the simple sensations, that as Berkeley says, their *"esse"* is "percipi"—their being is to be perceived or known. But that which perceives, or knows, is termed mind or spirit; and therefore the knowledge which the senses give is, after all, a knowledge of spiritual phenomena.

Professor Arthur Burtt, Professor of Philosophy at Cornell University, adds:

> The so-called higher mental powers of human persons seem to be the completest perspectives of reality so far as revealed in our experience; as Aristotle insisted, they include all that other orders of being do and more beside. . . . I had almost introduced the word "spirit" here, forgetting for a moment that at the sight of such a word sophisticated moderns would brand me at once a hopeless anachronism.

As a white, when I "see" a black man or woman, I am observing elements of only my own human being. As a black, when I "see" a white man or woman, I am observing elements of only my own human being. To illustrate, whenever I see my white American I see him in my mind. I understand that it is all his own living of his self that he calls his *"black"* American. Whenever I see my black American I see him in my mind. I understand that it is all his own living of his self that he calls his *"white"* American. *I cannot afford inobservance for this peace-making truth.*

Only I can live all or *any* of my living. My life *is* integrated, inviolably integrated. I can think only what I am; I can feel only what I am; and I can see or hear or otherwise sense only what I am. Such is the wholeness of human individuality.

I can help my self most by realizing that I am a *mind* individual, a *mind* person, and that it benefits me most to learn how to use safely the powerful mind of which I am composed. It is life-giving wisdom I have worked up for my self that reveals that I, only I, live and am responsible for the world I create in my mind.

"This is the great error of our day in the treatment of the human body," observed Plato twenty-five hundred years ago, "that physicians separate the soul from the body." An operational definition of man is that he is a biological whole, ultimately capable of cultivating his divine consciousness for the life-giving and lifesaving meaning of his wholeness-power. My science of man must be a science of my whole man, tap the immense resources of vitality on this *wholeness* plane. Meanwhile whatever I cannot consider and acknowledge as entirely my own untrammelled living, *is* my potential evidence for the existence of my vast uncultivated unconscious being. Realizing how hard it is for me to discipline my resisting self to awaken, and to keep awake, to this enlightenment, I remind my self of Albert Jay Nock's reference to his Epstean's law, "Man tends always to satisfy his needs and desires with the least possible exertion."*

*See Nock's uniquely American *Memoirs of a Superfluous Man,* Harper and Brothers, 1943. His quotes are also propitious, for example Alexander Dumas' description of Necker's political finance, "Trying to organize prosperity by generalizing poverty."

In my opinion, every educational theory of mine that is not based on my conviction that I, including every one of my world, am always exactly as I ought to be, must prove abortive. My fundamental semantic need, underlying every other one, is to observe my self meaning in my every word. Thomas à Kempis noted in his *Imitation,* "The fewer there be who follow the way to heaven, the harder that way is to find."

Dr. Alexis Carrel's book entitled *Man the Unknown* records, "Moral sense is almost completely ignored by modern society." My interest in what I call "society," other than as being a product of my own imagining, must be at the cost of my conscious self responsibility. "Collective" behavior of any kind can be nothing but irresponsible individual behavior. Lenin put it well, "It is nonsense to make any pretense of reconciling the State and liberty." In his letter to Macon in 1821, Thomas Jefferson writes, "Our Government is now taking so steady a course as to show by what road it will pass to destruction, 'to wit: by consolidation first (i.e. centralization) and then corruption, its necessary consequence." Nietzsche warned his self about the unawakened self appreciation in appearing to become a "mass-man,"—an "organization man," or State's man of today. My rare insightful statesman differentiates his own real conception of his State from every illusion of its impersonal existence.

I have known a great peace ever since discovering that all of my individuality really *is* nothing but individuality. Especially, I realize I have been able to examine my mind, ever since I could renounce my illusion of being able to make some other kind of observation. Particularly, being a self "educator," I have spared my self immeasurable exertion by seeing that my education is a process of awakening to the wisdom of my human being, and not some kind of improvement of, or addition to, an otherwise more or less worthless wasteland of ignorance. Prior to this *conscious* finding of my self, I puzzled painfully about the unpredictable results of so-called learning, and cherished an illusion somehow one person might get at, or be gotten at by, another, at least "to *some* extent."

The one essential ingredient of the only government that is

really possible is that it be heeded perseveringly as a conscious self development both in its spirit and in its method. "Government is a contrivance of human wisdom to provide for human wants," said Burke. "Human" implies self interest. Conscious self cultivation enables adequate American citizenship training. Whatever I consciously will to live is American in the truest sense of the word.

Self willed growth of self knowledge, is my definition of scientific education. No other kind of "consistent nomenclature" ("classified knowledge") can provide an adequate "scientific" substitute for the scientific exactness provided by duly self observed self experience. Only tenacious self consciousness enables me to, as Pope pictured it, "hold the eel of science by the tail."

For me, it is most costly self help to have to deny my personal identity in my political science, or in any of my so-called "external" world. All of "language of politics" is my instrument of thought, categorized as "politics." Consideration of the helpfulness of the mind cultured to become awake to its self is an issue second to none in human importance. Extension of my recognition of my identity decides the volitional range of my mind and, more vitally significant, sets the limits of appreciation for my life itself. Insight into the nature of my most inclusive way of identifying myself is both my most comprehensive and my most practical insight. Self consciousness is free mindedness. The kind of "scientific mindedness" which I consider to be ideal is entirely favorable to my free (conscious) creation of my imaginings. I find that the important truth about any of my living can be considered only through my imagination. By conscious *thinking* I can escape unconscious "doing."

Language is not a form of magic, not some kind of mystic word complex, which enables "communication." "Communication" is a myth, an ever popular fairy tale nearly always unrecognized as such. The real function of my word is to help me organize my life, direct my power, and understand my self. I live, create, my all. I cannot understand "another person." I cannot "impart" my language to "another," any more than I can impart my voice or hearing, dumbness or deafness, to him. A word is a symbol of a meaning, and meaning occurs nowhere except in an individual mind. John Locke was awake to the self concealing power of all language that is unrecognized as one's idiolect:

> Vague and insignificant forms of speech and abuse of language have so long passed for mysteries of science, and hard or misapplied words, with little or no meaning, have been. . . . mistaken for deep learning. They are but the covers of ignorance and hindrance of true knowledge.

Besides its significance for phantasy or day dreaming, my term "imagination" describes all creative use of my mind. I recognize and renounce the false but fearsome distinction that would oppose "imaginary" to *real*. Such effort at belittling this vitally productive power is intended to strengthen the mind by focusing its attention on illusional "external objectivity," but at the awful expense of distracting attention from the entirely subjective reality of the intact wholeness of the individual.

I find great helpfulness in rescuing my constantly inventive imagination from any and all askance. My only freedom, freedom of my mind, is based solidly upon my free use of this source of meaningful originality. Sanity, itself, can only be imagined sanity. If I cannot imagine my government to be my own, I must imagine my self as subject to it, rather than it as subject to me.

Particularly with respect to my highest ideals, I find it prudent to observe that my idea of so-called "opposites," implies an illusion of plurality. Whatever is, must be its own opposite. "Good" derives its meaning from "bad," and the converse. Aristotle saw, "The knowledge of opposites is one."

In the sense that it represents the only trustworthy method for setting up and maintaining government based upon the only real sovereignty, namely, that of the human individual, democracy is the true American ideal way of life. It is indeed rare for an American citizen to attain this kind of civic insight, but this painful observation in no way detracts from the indispensable factual worth for *peaceful human existence* of full measured conscious self possession and conscious self government. What Milton calls "the barbarous ignorance of the schools" I must acknowledge as my own also. Montaigne's tolerance I may make my very own possession, if I will, "O what a soft, easy, and wholesome pillow is ignorance and incuriosity whereon to compose a well-contrived head!"

Being a black or white, I need not despair of my chance to live the benefits of my full American citizenship in my lifetime. I can enjoy this privilege and opportunity just and only as soon as I make up my mind to do so, by enduring the shock of discovering my *whole* mind is *all* mine.

Although it may be true that I, a "black," may have to live my self in the one sure way to develop full realization that I *am* my only "white" or whatever "else," it is equally true that I, a "white," am under exactly the same necessity to obey the corresponding inexorable law of my health, and thus grow the American courage and honesty to declare, "I am my only black."

While this consciously humanizing process continues, timed according to the law of each one's natural individual growth, it is extremely helpful to realize that neither "black" nor "white" need wait upon his "other one" for his *immediate* realization of his heart's desire springing from his driving necessity to see his self as his whole, complete, all-loving, and all-including, world of his self. This farsighted world view of my Americanization is my reality. Helping my self by creating it *is* what my mind is for. *All* of my mental functioning is my biological process.

My willing my mind to work up exactly the kind of mental world I wish to call my own, will always remain my exclusive health responsibility no matter how seemingly ideal my so-called "external world" may actually seem to become through my efforts, including the efforts of my fellowman, to change "it." *It is precisely from shunning such full use of my mind that all of my symptoms of irresponsible violence derive.*

I can never fear or be angry with my fellowman, despite all appearance to the contrary. "I am angry," localizes my feeling exactly in my self, even if it does seem to eclipse all else that I am. All of my fear or anger *is,* and can only be, about its self alone and a warning for my whole self alone. It can apply to my fellowman absolutely no more than can any other feeling of pain I suffer. I must imagine my fellowman's pain or sorrow or anger to the extent that I see *my* fellowman *is* mine. *Only by intention-*

ally exciting my further self awareness can I avoid seeming to be subject to my emotions or to my reasoning.

My due regard for the conscious individualization process inherent in my American democracy necessitates my entirely new orientation to my mind. For example, I find it helpful to renounce all "duality" in favor of *unity,* all "difference" in favor of *sameness,* all "otherness" in favor of *selfness,* all "objectivity" in favor of subjectivity, and so on. Similarly, I discover powerful practicality in discerning the single-minded *identity* underlying the double-minded "separation" customarily made between "thinking" and "doing".

It is far easier to "act out" than to "think up" the idea of democratic individuality. Contrary to one's established belief, it can be easier to "do" than to "think." Evidently it requires huge conscious responsibility for me to "think up" my fellowman's behaving in a "hateful" way, whereas I can *appear* to "act" with my fellowman without assuming any responsibility for his behavior. However, "thinking" is a *doing* of thinking, quite as "doing" is a thinking of doing. "Thinking" is unconscious *doing* and "doing" is unconscious *thinking.* This important reality is rarely appreciated, but it enabled the profoundly humane thought attributable to each American's Thomas Jefferson to find expression in that one's uncritical democratic "action" without his having to take the trouble to *think* it responsibly into being.

I note well that my awakening to self sovereignty of my American democracy is a *difficultly* aroused trend of mental development. By putting on my sheep's clothing of the seeming practicality in "joining my fellowmen," I can avoid my idealistically and liberally putting on the new manfulness of waking up fully in order to see that I *am* all of my fellowman experiences. My materialistic view of my self confines me within the outlines of my physique. Then by human "individuality" I must limit my meaning, "the figure of a man," so that it does not include his world. My idealistic view of my self subsumes my materialistic one, but also enables me to observe all of *my* world as my meaningful individuality. Every American may love his life as an adventure in conscious self discovery. It is only self insightful for me to speak of "my" United States or "my" Declaration of Independence, just as of "my" blood, breath or being of every kind.

Certainly I find it most worthy but also most difficult to think responsibly of all of my "doing," if I am to understand my personal responsibility to extend to my awareness for my fellowman's doing. On the other hand, I can allow my self inordinate license in my "doing," if I understand it to exclude my personal responsibility for my fellowman's behavior. I am not merely my brother's keeper, I *am my* brother. It is not difficult to understand how my false dichotomy of "thinking" and "doing" established itself, when I consider the freedom it *appears* to give me to claim irresponsibility for my living of my fellowman. My Hindu divines,

> O Son of Spirit, I have created thee rich. How is it thou art poor? And made thee mighty. How is it thou art weak? And from the very essence of Love and Wisdom I have manifested thee. How is it thou occupiest thyself with someone else?

I am sensitively mindful of the perilous beginnings of my United States, traceable specifically to attaining and maintaining that indispensable source of power: *acknowledged unity.* Unquestionably it may seem easier for me to vote without awakening to the full meaning of my vote, or to "belong to a party" without realizing *my party belongs to me.* It was his devotion to his country's independence as his own that led Thomas Jefferson to declare while still minister to France:

> I never submitted the whole system of my opinions to the creed of any party of men whatever in religion, in philosophy, in politics, or in anything else where I was capable of thinking for myself. Such an addiction is the last degradation of a free and moral agent. If I could not go to heaven but with a party, I would not go there at all.

Rather than being based upon "freedom from" any of my life's meaning, my liberty is based upon my worked up appreciation for the importance of my *every* life meaning. <u>First</u> I must tolerate or consent to whatever I experience, before I can live it 

with my proper self love. Life endurance for whatever I experience, is my primary demand. Freedom to live my experience as desirable often must come later. My conscious personal identity is founded upon my consent, or wish to claim it; my "depersonalized" being is founded upon my dissent, or wish to disclaim it.

Insightlessly claimed support for the sufficiency of human individuality may be used by me to cover a multitide of attempts at violation of my human individuality. Although surely a democratic rule in its intention, it is certainly true that my "rule of the majority" can operate as a kind of mob rule. Furthermore, it must operate thus as (illusional) "mob rule" to the extent that my voting is not consciously derived from the overall human truth of the sovereignty of my (including my fellow citizen's) human self.

In order that a political writer may distinguish himself in his treatment of the essence of the democratic ideal of living, it is essential that he understand the meaning of freedom itself. For that understanding he must be able to renounce the fear of unrelieved human individuality. By "unrelieved individuality" is meant: that comprehension of human creaturehood which conceives it to be its own everything, its own all, its own universe. In his famous literary exchange with Walter Lippman, Archibald MacLeish, mind conscious American citizen that he is, states this case with the wonderful unity of expression which is conferred only by respected mental integration.* "Ever-increasing consciousness, which means ever-increasing individual consciousness, which means ever-increasing individuality, is the law of human gravity and it cannot be reversed." Again, "Man's journey is a journey from the remote insensibility of the jelly of his biological beginnings toward the fulfillment of consciousness, and the fulfillment of consciousness is an individual, not a herd, achievement." And again, "We no longer assume the superior reality of the public world of objective reason. We assume instead the deeper reality of the world within—which is

---

*MacLeish and Lippman, "On the Public Philosophy," *Perspectives,* No. 14, Winter 1956, pp. 160–162, Intercultural Publications Inc. of New York. Published in Great Britain by Hamish Hamilton Ltd., 90 Great Russell Street, London, W. C. 1

to say, the world which each human individual uniquely is." And finally, "The postulates which will give us peace are not the postulates which satisfy us on another coast. They are the postulates which will express our life beyond—our life as individual human beings set free to be ourselves."

Poet, physician, prelate, or ideal patriot,—each identifies his manpower with this conscious self knowledge: 1) consciousness is the humanizing power of man, and 2) all consciousness is self consciousness.

My every individual is of necessity *always* independent, but only rarely does one realize (imagine) this precious truth. Duly, therefore, I make my Declaration of *Conscious* Independence:

> *I, including my every fellowman, am born, live all of my life, and die, one only but entirely self contained individual. All I can ever really be "lonesome for" is my appreciation for my united wholeness. I can never really be at a loss except for my recognition of my complete and intact fullness. My life provides my only possible reality. My inability to see my personal identity in any of my world is traceable to my need to sleep through it. My acknowledging my personal identity in any of my living is traceable to my arousing my self to be wide awake to it. I can never "have" anything; I must always be everything. My only possible consciousness is self consciousness; my only possible unconsciousness is self unconsciousness. My vicissitudes in the condition of my self love create controls directing my being. My only possible governing power is acknowledgeable or unacknowledgeable self sovereignty. My insight regarding my absolute autonomy is the consequence of my willingly waking up sufficiently to be able to call my soul my own and my all my soul.*

My God! how little do my country men know what precious blessings they are in possession of and which no other people on earth enjoy.
Thomas Jefferson to James Monroe,
April 15, 1785

Theodore Roosevelt

INDEX

KEY TO DECLARATION OF INDEPENDENCE
BY JOHN TRUMBULL

1. George Wythe.
2. William Whipple.
3. Joseph Bartlett.
4. Thomas Lynch.
5. Benjamin Harrison.
6. Richard Henry Lee.
7. Samuel Adams.
8. George Clinton.
9. William Paca.
10. Samuel Chase.
11. Richard Stockton.
12. Lewis Morris.
13. William Floyd.
14. Arthur Middleton.
15. Thomas Heyward, Jr.
16. Charles Carroll.
17. Robert Morris.
18. Thomas Willing.
19. Benjamin Rush.
20. Elbridge Gerry.
21. Robert Treat Paine.
22. William Hooper.
23. Stephen Hopkins.
24. William Ellery.
25. George Clymer.
26. Joseph Hewes.
27. George Walton.
28. James Wilson.
29. Abraham Clark.
30. Francis Hopkinson.
31. John Adams.
32. Roger Sherman.
33. Robert R. Livingston.
34. Thomas Jefferson.
35. Benjamin Franklin.
36. Thomas Nelson, Jr.
37. Francis Lewis.
38. John Witherspoon.
39. Samuel Huntington.
40. William Williams.
41. Oliver Wolcott.
42. Charles Thomson.
43. John Hancock.
44. George Read.
45. John Dickinson.
46. Edward Rutledge.
47. Thomas McKean.
48. Philip Livingston.

GALLERY OF FINE ARTS · YALE UNIVERSITY